HAPPINESS
in
HARD TIMES

written and illustrated by
Andrew Matthews

HAY HOUSE
Australia • Canada • Hong Kong • India
South Africa • United Kingdom • United States

First published and distributed in the United Kingdom by:
Hay House UK Ltd, Astley House, 33 Notting Hill Gate, London W11 3JQ.
Tel.:+44 (0)20 3675 2450; Fax:+44 (0)20 3675 2451. www.hayhouse.co.uk

Published and distributed in the United States of America by:
Hay House, Inc., PO Box 5100, Carlsbad, CA 92018-5100. Tel.: (1) 760 431 7695
or (800) 654 5126; Fax: (1) 760 431 6948 or (800) 650 5115. www.hayhouse.com

Published and distributed in Australia by:
Hay House Australia Ltd, 18/36 Ralph St, Alexandria NSW 2015. Tel.: (61) 2
9669 4299; Fax: (61) 2 9669 4144. www.hayhouse.com.au

Published and distributed in the Republic of South Africa by:
Hay House SA (Pty), Ltd, PO Box 990, Witkoppen 2068. Tel./Fax: (27) 11 467
8904. www.hayhouse.co.za

Distributed in Canada by:
Raincoast, 9050 Shaughnessy St, Vancouver, BC V6P 6E5. Tel.: (1) 604 323 7100;
Fax: (1) 604 323 2600

© Andrew Matthews, 2009, 2010

The moral rights of the author have been asserted.

The author of this book does not dispense medical advice or prescribe the use of
any technique as a form of treatment for physical or medical problems without
the advice of a physician, either directly or indirectly. The intent of the author
is only to offer information of a general nature to help you in your quest for
emotional and spiritual wellbeing. In the event you use any of the information
in this book for yourself, which is your constitutional right, the author and the
publisher assume no responsibility for your actions.

A catalogue record for this book is available from the British Library.

This title was previously published by Seashell Publishers, Australia,
ISBN 978-0-9757642-0-6.

ISBN 978-1-84850-248-2

Printed and bound in Great Britain by
TJ International, Padstow, Cornwall.

To the millions of readers of our books all over the world...

I don't know where to begin or what to say, or how to express our gratitude for your loyalty, generosity and daily emails, because a mere *thank you* doesn't seem enough.

Andrew and I are overwhelmed and ever so grateful to you for keeping in touch with us. I want you to know that every email that you send us is read and appreciated. Thank you from the depths of our hearts.

To my dear friend Michael Rakuson – former director of Tower Books – thank you for encouraging me to produce *Happiness in Hard Times*. In your quiet, gentle manner, you persuaded me to create a book appropriate for the current times. Bless you, Michael.

To all of you who responded with your stories when I asked for help, I thank you with all my heart. You replied so graciously and promptly. You sent us thousands of emails. Each of your stories continues to inspire Andrew and me. I admire your strength and courage. I congratulate you on deciding to move forward, seeking happiness in spite of your challenges. This is the book you all helped to write, for everyday people going through everyday challenges.

To Annie Backhaus, Adrian Elmer, Alfred Engel, Mark Kenway, Geoff McClure, Rod Mudgway, Dianne Mulcahy, Moya Mulvay, Cherry Parker, Jenny Truran – to Alison, Craig, Greg, Hong, Joe, Carmen, Frank and Maria, thank you for sharing your experiences.

You bared your souls so courageously. You opened your hearts each time we spoke. You held nothing back. You shared your stories in the hope that your stories would inspire one other person to feel better. To all of you, I salute you!!

And to you the reader...this is the book for everyday people going through everyday challenges. This book is for you. This is a book for your friends, your family, your colleagues, your neighbours. This is a book for people you meet on your travels and for people you know who are going through troubled times.

Happiness in Hard Times is also a book for those of us who haven't been through hard times. It puts your life into perspective. It will get you back on track. It will make you realise that a better and brighter future is waiting – and remind you how to get there.

Happiness in Hard Times will inspire so, so many readers.

Your journey to peace and happiness has already begun. I wish you all life's very best

Julie

Julie M Matthews

CONTENTS

Acceptance

On a bicycle ride around the world, my friend Aden stopped awhile in a West African village to help build a bakery. He said:

It took us several months to build the bakery. We made the bricks from crushed anthills. Every day the village children came to help. None of the kids had shoes but one happy little guy always wore one sock – no shoes, just a sock. He was about 10 years old. I called him One Sock.

Eventually my curiosity got the better of me. I said, "One Sock, tell me about this sock you always wear."

He said proudly, "My Mum washes it every night. I wear it every day."

I said, "Yes, but why do you wear one?"

He seemed surprised by my silly question, and then he smiled broadly and said, "Because I only have one!"

Perhaps you are broke right now. Perhaps you have lost your job or lost a loved one. Maybe you are sick. You say, "I just don't know what to do."

Here is the first thing to do – and the only thing to do.

You accept where you are.

To turn things around you first make peace with your situation. Forget about blame, forget about guilt, forget the "what ifs." Progress depends on acceptance. Acceptance doesn't mean, "I want to stay here." Acceptance means: "This is where I am – and now I move on to what I want."

Instead of, "My husband is a gorilla and I'm stuck with him," it is more like, "My husband is a gorilla. What a perfect learning experience! I now realise I deserve better treatment."

Instead of, "I've lost all my money. If only I hadn't invested everything with Honest Eddie's Equity Fund," you say, "I am where I am. I made it once, I'll make it again."

Imagine you are overweight and you want to become thin. If you say:

- I'm not fat, or
- it's my mother's fault that I am fat, or
- my sister is *fatter.*

What happens? You stay fat.

But there's another option:

- *I am fat. I like myself whether or not I'm fat. I now choose to lose 50 kilos.*

You accept where you are. Now you can move forward.

Acceptance isn't *giving up.* Acceptance is recognition that, "This is a part of my journey." Very often it means, "Right now *I have no idea* why this had to be a part of my journey but I embrace it anyway."

In a Nutshell
Acceptance is power.

Quick Quiz:

Imagine that in the last week you:

- tattooed your backside
- thumped your neighbour
- got married
- robbed a bank
- donated a kidney
- had botox
- joined a monastery
- devoured a huge pizza in three minutes *and*
- leaped off a very high bridge.

Okay, so you had a busy week.

Question: What do each of the above have in common?

Answer: These are all things that you might do to feel happier. Really! In fact, it's a trick question because I could have put *anything* on the list. The motivation behind *everything* you do – and the motivation behind *everything everybody does* – is to feel better.

Don't take my word for it. Ask the psychologists or read Plato, Aristotle and Sigmund Freud. There is a lot of debate about *the meaning of life*. There is broad agreement about *why we do what we do* – we want to be happy and stay happy.

You devour an entire pizza in three minutes. Your

thought is, "This feels good. I want to be happy now." You hire a personal trainer and eat lettuce for six months. Your aim is, "I want to like my butt – and this will make me happier." You quit alcohol. Why? "If I do this I will feel better." Whether you donate to Red Cross or belt your neighbour, your motive is, "If I do this I will feel better."

Mary says, "I donate to charity because I want to help people." Sure, Mary, but would you donate if it made you miserable? Fred says, "I punched my neighbour because he came at me with a spade!" Correct, Fred. You made a hasty decision, "To be happier in the very short term I need to break Larry's nose before he whacks me with a gardening tool."

Different people do *different things* but the objective remains the same – *if I do this I will feel better.*

You study accountancy for four years to please your Dad. You say, "I did it to make *him* happy." No you didn't. You did it because you feel better *doing what he wants* than you would feel *doing what you want.*

Whether you sacrifice for your kids, whether you marry or divorce, whether you get a tattoo or join the priesthood, the ultimate goal is the same. Even if you leap off a very high bridge, it is an attempt to feel better – "I'll be happier dead than alive."

Is it Selfish to Pursue Happiness?

Here's what's crazy. We all chase happiness – it's automatic – but some people worry that it is selfish. So they feel guilty – and that makes them unhappy!

It's not selfish to seek happiness. IT IS SELFISH TO BE MISERABLE! Happy people are more thoughtful and more considerate. It's *unhappy people* who are preoccupied with *themselves*. Happy people make better friends, better lovers and better employees.

"They're not happy. They just THINK they're happy."

Studies prove that if you are happy you are more likely to:
- volunteer at a soup kitchen
- carry a stranger's groceries or
- loan people money.

If you are miserable you are more likely to:
- complain about your ulcer
- steal from your boss or
- kick a dog.

So for the sake of everyone you know – and for the benefit of all the dogs in your neighbourhood – let's get one thing straight: the *happier* you become, the better off *we all* will be!

Hard times can mean *no money*. Hard times can

mean *no friends, no job* and *no hope.* Hope is what we need most. The good news is that it is possible for you to climb out of the deepest hole. If you are unhappy with your life right now, you may look back in a few months and see how these difficult times helped to prepare you for something better.

Most of us start out life believing:

- mistakes are bad
- the happiest people have the easiest lives
- the smartest people are the most successful
- we need a partner to be happy.

None of the above statements are necessarily true.

I Can't Take it Anymore!

Sometimes life is hard. How do you hang on when things seem hopeless? You can only tackle your problems as you would climb a mountain.

If you go rock climbing and you get stuck on a ledge, you suddenly focus on the present moment! When your life is in danger, you forget about the future. All your effort goes into your next step. Then your next step. Inch by inch. Eventually you claw your way out.

The same strategy works for everyday life. It is the *only strategy* when life gets tough. You say, "How can I stay positive when I can't even pay the rent? How do I keep going when I'm grieving, lonely or seriously ill?"

When the worst happens, you can't worry about the *rest of your life.* You can't even be worrying about the *rest of the month.* But you can usually handle one day at a time. And whenever 24 hours is too tough, bite off five minutes at a time. Tackle one problem at a time.

Take a step. You get a little confidence... take another step, and another. Eventually you find that the worst is over.

If you were to worry about:

a) everything you need to do in the next month, or

b) everything that could go wrong in the next year, you could go nuts! Focus on the moment.

If you were embarking on a day's march, wouldn't it be foolish to try to carry enough food and water for a lifetime? Is it not strange, then, that many people carry around all their worries for the next 25 years and wonder why life is so difficult? We were designed to live 24 hours at a time. No more.

Next time you find yourself despairing, ask yourself:

- have I got enough air to breathe?
- have I got enough food for today?
- will I be okay for the next five minutes?

Once you have made it through those five minutes, just aim at getting through the next five. Bite off one small chunk at a time. It saves a lot of indigestion.

In a Nutshell
All you can do is give your best effort until bedtime.
Let tomorrow take care of itself.

Hong's Story

I met Sushma in Singapore in 1982. I was 33 years old and she was 18. She was the daughter of an Indian father and a Chinese mother – and beautiful. For 15 years I had travelled the world. I had girlfriends but never considered marriage. I knew within five minutes of meeting Sushma that she would be my wife, and we married within a year.

I had an electronics trading business in Spain at the time and Sushma moved there with me. In March 1987 our only son, Jordi, was born. We lived in Europe until he was four years old. When my work took me to Nigeria we decided that it would be safest – and best for Jordi's education – if he and Sushma moved to Singapore.

It was while I was in Nigeria, on 23 May 1991, that I received a 2 a.m. telephone call from my friends at my office. Sushma had been in an accident in Singapore – her car had hit a tree on Bukit Timah Rd. Hoping for the best, I packed my bags to return home, but within hours I received a second call with the news that Sushma had died. I went crazy. I cried and cried for weeks. I cried that I had lost my wife – but most of all I cried for my four-year-old son. How would Jordi manage without his mother? How would I raise him?

My first commitment to my son was that I would never marry again until he was an adult. I decided that Jordi should continue to live and be educated in Singapore. He stayed with his grandparents during school. During vacations he joined me in Africa and Europe.

We travelled the world as buddies – to Germany, Austria, South Africa and Brazil. He was my fun-loving best friend, my companion, my soul mate. Together we discovered a world that he could never find in books.

Another Phone Call

I moved to Bali in 2001 to start a new life and create the business I have now. Jordi loved coming to Bali for his vacations. By mid 2006 Jordi finished high school and came to stay with me. He wanted a motor bike and I bought him one as a graduation present.

Then on 20 September the police called me at 2 a.m. Jordi had had an accident. By the time I arrived at the hospital he was already blue. He died within ten minutes. He was 19.

First my wife, then my son.

I was numb. My entire world collapsed. I walked in the forest for four days, in a daze. Everywhere I went I saw Jordi. I took a trip to Thailand to try to heal. Still I would see him. I returned to Bali and on the anniversary of the 40th day, we held a church ceremony for him.

The months went by and, slowly, I began to live my life again. Perhaps my 13 years in Africa helped me to deal with my loss. The European says, "This should not have happened!" The African says, "It happened. Life goes on." I could say, "Why did I allow him to ride that bike?" But would that help?

If through sadness you can fix the future, then do it! But being sad doesn't fix the future.

I have no regrets. I did everything I could with my son. I gave him the most I could give. And my life now? I am an artist. I create, I carve. I enjoy animals. I enjoy the people I meet. All my possessions I value at nothing.

> "If through sadness you can fix the future, then do it! But being sad doesn't fix the future."

You never know how you will react to tragedy. It's like when you imagine a tiger jumping through your window. You say, "If a tiger leaped into my living room, I would do this!" But when the real tiger arrives, you do something totally different.

I wake up every day choosing to be happy. What can possibly hurt me now? What can worry me now? Life is like a movie. It's not the length but the quality that matters.

There is no secret to happiness. You just choose it.

Why Is Life So Hard?

We learn most in life when we get hit over the back of the head. Why? Because it's easier *not* to change. So we keep doing what we're doing until it becomes too painful.

Take our health for example. When do we change diets and start exercising? When our body is falling apart – when the doctor says, "If you don't change your lifestyle, you'll kill yourself!" Suddenly we're motivated!

In relationships: when do we usually tell each other how much we care? When the marriage is falling apart, when the family is falling apart!

In school: when do we finally knuckle down and study? When we're about to fail.

In business: when do we try new ideas and make the tough decisions? When we can't pay our bills. When do we finally learn about customer service? After the customers have left!

We learn our biggest lessons when things get rough. When have you made the most important decisions in your life? When you were on your knees – after disasters, after knock-backs, when you've been kicked in the head! That's when we say to ourselves, "I'm sick of being broke, I'm tired of being mediocre. I'm going to do something."

Success we celebrate – but we don't learn too much. Failure hurts – and that's when we get educated. In retrospect, we usually notice that "disasters" were turning points.

Why Me?

When tragedy strikes, or when we lose everything, or when a lover walks out on us, the question we usually ask is "WHY? WHY me? WHY now? WHY did she leave me for a loser?" Asking "WHY?" questions can send us crazy. Often, there is no answer to "WHY?" Or it doesn't matter why!

Effective people ask "WHAT?" questions, "WHAT do I learn from this? WHAT am I going to do about it?" When the situation is really desperate, they ask, "WHAT can I do, just today, to make things better?"

Effective people don't go looking for problems, but when they get smacked in the mouth, they ask themselves, "*How do I need to change what I'm thinking and what I'm doing? How can I be better than I am now?*" Losers ignore all the warning signs. When the roof falls in, they ask, "Why does everything happen to me?"

We are creatures of habit. We keep doing what we're doing until we're forced to change.

Mary gets dumped by boyfriend Al. Devastated, she locks herself in her bedroom for a week. Then gradually she starts to call old friends and meet new ones. She soon moves house and changes jobs. Within six months she is happier and more confident than she has ever been in her life. She looks back on the "disaster" of losing Al as the best thing that ever happened to her.

Fred gets the sack. Unable to find work, he starts his own little business. For the first time in his life he is his own boss, and doing what he really wants to do. He still has his problems, but his life has new meaning and excitement – and all out of apparent disaster.

So is life a series of painful disasters?

Not necessarily. The universe is always nudging us with gentle signals. When we ignore the signals, it nudges us with a sledgehammer. Growth is most painful when we resist it.

We can react to life in one of three ways. We either say:

- "MY LIFE IS A SERIES OF EXPERIENCES I NEED, HAPPENING IN PERFECT ORDER." (The healthiest approach – guarantees maximum peace of mind.)
- "LIFE IS A LOTTERY, BUT I MAKE THE MOST OF WHATEVER COMES ALONG." (The next best option – offers average quality of life.)
- "WHY DO BAD THINGS ALWAYS HAPPEN TO ME?" (Guarantees maximum misery and frustration.)

Life goes like this. We get hit by little pebbles – as a kind of warning. When we ignore the pebbles, we get hit by a brick. Ignore the brick and we get wiped out by a boulder. If we're honest, we can see where we have ignored the warning signs. And then we have the nerve to say, "Why me?"

Life doesn't always have to be painful – but pain is still the main reason we change. Until we are in pain, we can pretend. Our ego says, "I'm fine."

It's always easier to be philosophical about *other people's pain!* We look at Jim and say, "Going broke was a huge learning experience for him." We look at Mary and say, "That divorce helped her to stand on her own feet." We all agree, "Challenges make you stronger."

But when our own challenges come along, we're not so enthusiastic. We say, "Lord, why this? Give me a *convenient* challenge!" Unfortunately, real challenges aren't convenient.

ANDREW MATTHEWS

Challenges also come in waves. We know about waves – sound waves, light waves, brain waves, microwaves. In non-scientific terms waves demonstrate that *things have a tendency to travel in bunches.*

This means that problems happen in groups; family crises, wedding invitations and car repairs also tend to travel in bunches. Bearing this in mind is helpful. When you strike a month without bills, you say to yourself, *"I'll put something aside for the next wave."* When you get swamped by the next wave, you say to yourself, *"I know about these waves – this is only temporary."*

Adrian's Story

It was a cold, starlit night in 2006 and I was wandering down a country lane in my village. I have always found such clear nights comforting, but not that night. The sky looked very, very large, planet earth seemed like a mere speck, and I was just one lonely soul amongst billions of strangers.

I felt a failure and a lousy father. Through my tears I counted all the reasons why people should despise me. "Why should anyone respect me when I hate myself? Who would care if I lived or died?"

> "I had my dog's heavy choker around my neck and I was looking for a place to hang myself."

I had my dog's heavy choker lead around my neck and I was looking for a place to hang myself.

By the side of the road there was a telegraph pole, and on the pole, about 12 feet above the ground there was fixed a heavy horizontal beam. I could hang myself from that beam! I gathered together some wooden pallets and miscellaneous rubbish into a pile and climbed on top, but no matter how I rearranged the pile, I couldn't quite reach that beam. So I went home to get a stepladder.

When I arrived home I found my Labrador, Jack, waiting for me at the front door. He was so pleased to see me! He jumped and danced, and did that silly little run he does – across the lawn and around the bush and back – over and over again.

In that moment I realised, "*I do make a difference to one living creature.*" Jack's warm welcome lifted me. I thought, "Maybe I should take this leash from around my throat and feed him his dinner!" And I thought, "If I make a difference to a dog, maybe I can be of use to someone – anyone." I never collected the stepladder.

My Business Goes Belly-Up

How did I get so low? It wasn't so much *what* happened, but that *so much* happened in one year. I had an old friend, Ted, who was a brilliant digital artist and we decided to start a web business to market his work. We needed cash to launch our venture so I borrowed money against my house. After an enthusiastic start, Ted got fed up and moved to Spain.

When a business is going bad, you get clues, like:

* When you find yourself going through the pockets of every old pair of trousers and searching down the back of every chair for loose change.
* When the only food in your house is a jar of pickles and a half bottle of ketchup.
* When you are racking your brain to figure out, "What amazing dish can I create with a jar of pickles and a half bottle of ketchup?"

Deep Depression

It was at that time that my mother died of leukaemia and that hit me very hard. I knew Mum was sick but I never thought we would lose her. Then, whilst I was grieving for my Mum, the bank repossessed my home.

It's a long story. I fought to keep the house and nearly did – but in the end the courts ruled against me and I had an hour to race home and remove as much stuff as I could before the bailiff changed the locks and I was homeless. Luckily, a couple of good friends took me in and gave me a roof over my head until I could find somewhere else to live.

Nature's law is that the weak get bullied. As fragile as I was, it is no surprise that I found a truck-driving job where the boss berated and abused me, Monday to Friday. We were a perfect match – I needed the money and he needed someone to scream at.

My depression got deeper. This was not some kind of "blue day" blues – but a deep, debilitating, crushing helplessness. Forty-two-tonne-truck drivers are meant to be tough, but I couldn't make it through a day without crying uncontrollably. When people came to see me at my house I would hide. Most of my friends and family gave up on me and that's when I found myself on that lonely road with a noose round my neck.

Fortunately my dog saved me and then the doctors did their bit. I was diagnosed with acute anxiety and severe depression, and prescribed strong drugs. Wary of the drugs, I tried counselling and herbal medicine first, but eventually I took the recommended medication.

I survived on the heavy drugs for two years but only just. My mind was a fog, as if I was half drunk and half demented. I couldn't remember the simplest things, I couldn't speak properly – even recalling everyday words was a struggle. The doctors warned me against coming off the drugs, but the cure was worse than the disease! Eventually I had to quit the tablets. Whether I learned to live without them or whether I killed myself in the process, it seemed like win–win.

Doing it My Way

I threw away my pills and waited for the crash, but it never came. I began to live drug-free and that victory made me stronger. I started reading books on self-help, psychology and psychiatry. I learned that worrying about the past and fretting about the future were futile – that my mission was to handle the present.

A chance encounter with a hypnotherapist on a train provided the final link in the chain. He treated me and gave me tools to counter negative thoughts and tools to enhance my appreciation of everything I had.

Although my children never heard the whole story, I have been touched by their concern. I will never forget being lectured to by my ten-year-old, "You must take your pills! It's important, Dad," he said waving his stubby little finger at me. "I don't want to have to grow up without you!"

Nowadays I take time to do things that give me joy. I write comedy sketches for my own pleasure and post them on a blog. I write for the fun of it – no matter if my work is never published. I also make a point of recognising ways in which I make a difference to the lives of people that I meet daily – not out of ego, but out of appreciation. When life is getting a little grey again, I remind myself that I do matter to someone, somewhere, and this means there will be others that I can touch tomorrow. And so I need to find out what tomorrow holds – every tomorrow!

I meet with a group of friends regularly, and just last week, one of the ladies said, "Adrian, do you know what you give us all?"

Naively, I said, "No idea."

She said, "When we are around you, we feel special. We feel loved."

Her comment was the greatest gift. If my only legacy is that I have made some people feel loved, that is enough. One thing I have learned: you can't love other people until you can love yourself.

Today I'm back on top, I run my own company, I am happy. No matter how desperate things seem, there is a way back. I know. I was there and I came back.

Adrian's email: themanorfarm@btinternet.com

Step By Step

My wife Julie asked Adrian, "How did you feel and what were you thinking the night you tried to hang yourself?"

Adrian said, "I didn't feel anything. That was the problem. I had just spent the evening with my friends but I felt no connection with them or with anybody. Unless you have been there, you'll never know what it's like."

Adrian reminds us that progress happens in small steps. Look for good things, focus on the present and do what you can do today. As you change, so your life changes. Adrian explained, "There was no 'eureka' moment, no point at which I said, 'I'm cured.' It was just a slow process of realisation that I do matter, a slow process of taking control. And that's how *real life* often is – a steady process."

It's a Disaster!

Tom and Debbie are teenage lovers. Debbie gets pregnant at 16 and the entire family is distraught. It's a disaster!

Debbie decides to keep the child. She quits school to raise her son. Mum and Dad say, "She was such a brilliant student. What a disaster!"

Tom and Debbie get married at 18. They're unhappy, they fight. The family says, "It's a disaster."

They divorce at 22 and Debbie becomes a single Mum. All the neighbours say, "It's a disaster."

At 26 Debbie completes her degree in social work. She decides her mission is to help teenage mothers. She gets a job with a government agency and travels the country giving support and inspiration to young girls. Her son turns out to be the light of her life and her grandparents' pride and joy. At 28, Debbie marries the man of her dreams.

Debbie now has a beautiful son, a meaningful job, a loving husband and a strong relationship with her parents.

Quick quiz: Which bit was the disaster?

- Was it having the baby that became the joy of her life?
- Was it postponing her education to study something that she really cared about?
- Was it her first marriage that taught her what really matters in a relationship?

Did you ever look back on a bad relationship or a massive disappointment and say to yourself, "At the time it seemed like the worst thing that could have happened, but now I realise it was just what I needed."

If Not for This I'd Be Happy!

We have a lot of excuses for postponing happiness. Here are six:

Excuse No. 1: *If I were somewhere else, I'd be happy!*

We say, "Maybe if I go to a new city, I can make a new start!"

Take Fred, who owes money to half the neighbourhood. Fred says to himself, "Maybe I need to move!" But when he moves, he'll take his thoughts and habit patterns with him – and they are what shape his life. Fred changes cities and attracts the same situations, and another bunch of angry creditors.

If you're a spendthrift, and you migrate to Argentina, you'll still be a spendthrift. The best advice to Fred: *"Before changing your address, consider changing your thinking!"*

If only I could go to Tibet, maybe I could find the meaning of life...

Some of us get grand ideas about traveling to distant lands to find the meaning of life... Jim treks off to the Himalayas. One day, while sitting on a dusty street corner, racked with diarrhea and dreaming of a warm bath, he has a blinding flash, "Maybe I can 'do enlightenment' at the Ritz Carlton!"

It sounds romantic finding the meaning of life in Tibet, but enlightenment in Tibet is for Tibetans! The meaning of life for most of us is probably in the suburbs.

In a Nutshell

Usually, the best place to make a new start is where you are!

Excuse No. 2: *If I were older – or younger – I'd be happy!*

You think happiness depends on your age? In the 1990s researcher Ronald Inglehart published the results of a massive "happiness survey" involving 170,000 people from 16 countries. The participants were asked questions like, "How happy are you?" and "Are you satisfied with your life?"

Inglehart was interested to see whether our age affects our happiness. He analysed the data by age group: 15 to 24 years old, 25 to 34 years old, 35 to 44 years and so on. So who do you think were the most miserable? The teens? The mid-lifers? And who do you think were the happiest? Here are the results:

15–24 years	81% satisfied with life
25–34 years	80% satisfied with life
35–44 years	80% satisfied with life
45–54 years	79% satisfied with life
55–64 years	79% satisfied with life
65 years and over	81% satisfied with life

The results for each age group were almost identical!

In different research, Arizona State University psychologists William Stock and Morris Okun reached exactly the same conclusion. They assessed the results of over 100 psychological studies and boiled them down to this – that age has no more than a 1 per cent impact on happiness!

Despite all the myths, and despite all the talk of "troubled teens" and "mid-life crises," age has no real bearing on your happiness!

In a Nutshell

It's not about your age, it's about your attitude.

Excuse No. 3: *When I meet the perfect partner I'll be happy!*

If there is one thing we know about happy couples, it is this: happy people were happy *before* they met their partners.

No one else can ever MAKE you happy! Where do we get the idea that someone else can MAKE us happy? Maybe from songs and movies: in songs and movies people say, "Before you, I was lonely, I was a loser – but you changed everything!" But it's a myth. In the real world people say, "Before you, I was miserable – but YOU RUINED EVERYTHING!"

Happy people attract happy people. Miserable people attract miserable people. When you are feeling cheerful, do you ever say to yourself, "I should go find some gloomy people!"? You don't! You look for other happy people. Whatever you *are* is what you *get*. To be surrounded by positive people, you first put a smile on your own face.

If you are feeling down or depressed, only you can change your thoughts. Step by step, you pull yourself out of the hole. As you begin to look on the bright side, you attract happy friends and colleagues.

In a Nutshell

In the real world, other people
don't change our lives.
We do it ourselves.

"How do you live with this creep?"

Excuse No. 4: If I didn't have these problems I'd be happy!

You will always have problems – and when you haven't got big problems, little problems become big problems.

A retired executive told me, "I used to worry about million dollar takeovers. Now I get stressed out over dirty windows and lawn clippings!" He said, "Now that I have less major worries, I worry about minor things that don't matter." It's true. We find things to worry about.

Picture yourself on a 12-hour plane trip. You've just taken off, and you are hoping to relax and maybe even get some sleep. And then you notice it. The fellow next to you is sniffing, and he's doing it like clockwork, every six seconds. "One, two, three, four, five, *sniff*, one, two, three, four, five, *sniff*..." Oh no! This guy's a sniffing metronome! You say to yourself, "If I didn't have to put up with this turkey, I'd be happy!"

You take out your calculator, "Ten sniffs a minute multiplied by... that's seven thousand two hundred sniffs until Paris. This could be the worst night of my life!" Until now you hadn't noticed the sleeping baby behind you. But now he's wide awake and testing his lungs. Non-stop howling infants on non-stop flights are hard to ignore. This is when you say to yourself, "And I was worried about 'Sniffer!' I can tolerate bad manners, but wailing babies? No wonder I'm upset!"

It's about now that things take a turn for the worse. Without warning your jumbo jet shudders and plunges earthward. You feel the blood drain from your face as your stomach lodges in your throat. Everyone is screaming. Reaching for your life jacket you make a deal with God, "Get me out of this power dive and I'll never be irritated by sniffers again. I'll happily suffer screaming infants all the way to Europe."

The plane levels out and begins to climb. The captain apologises for the turbulence. Baby stops crying and Sniffer falls asleep. You resume your crossword in peace – and guess what! Sniffer starts to *snore*. "Oh no! If I didn't have to put up with this, I'd be happy!"

Here's how life is. We have a "worry hierarchy" and the most important things get worried about. While we've got a broken leg we don't worry about a headache – until the broken leg has healed. Snoring husbands are only irritating until the bedroom catches fire.

So how do we get less irritated? We recognise that our

stress is caused by rules in our own head. As we relax some of the rules, or drop them altogether, we become happier.

We make a conscious decision, "No one is going to ruin my day." We make a pact with ourselves that "No parking meter attendant, no traffic cop, no waitress with a chip on her shoulder is going to mess with my 24 hours." We remind ourselves that in the context of world events, a confrontation with a rude checkout clerk is not *that* dramatic.

In a Nutshell

There are alternatives to getting angry. It is possible to be fascinated or amused. The fewer rules you have about how life ought to be, and how other people ought to behave, the easier it is to be happy.

Excuse No. 5: *If only I had that!*

There is a bunch of people in the world dedicated to making you dissatisfied. They are tricky, even brilliant, and they operate with billion pound budgets! They use shame, guilt and humour to convince you that you are missing something. They will tell you that they have the solution to your happiness and make outrageous promises!

Are they the TV evangelists? Actually, I'm talking about *advertisers and marketers*. Their mission is to make you unhappy with *what you have* so you buy *what they have*:

Example: You bought a family car last year. It is pretty, it is roomy, it is safe – it even has six airbags.

You're very proud. Then you open the newspaper to discover that the latest model now has *11 air bags – for parents who care about their children!* "Oh no! I'm letting my family down!"

Example: You return from the supermarket and flick on the TV to discover that seven out of ten dentists recommend the toothpaste that you *didn't buy* and *happy cats* don't eat the crap that you just fed your kitty. (Even my cat isn't happy!) And because your toilet cleaner is second rate your entire bathroom is about to be swallowed up by bacteria. And you need Gucci to be cool and Rolex to look like a discerning achiever.

Advertisers target our ego – that part of us that loves to compare, "If you want to be suave, sophisticated, up-to-date, a good mother or the envy of your friends, you need this now."

When our self-worth is dependent on the stuff we own, we play a losing game. You buy a designer handbag. You are thrilled on day one, still pleased on days two and three, but by day ten the excitement has worn off. You ask yourself, "What can I buy next to make me feel better?"

Most of us own lots of stuff. Nothing wrong with that. The question is, "Why do we own it?"

My wife Julie has a lot of Chinese antique furniture, some of which she has owned for 30 years. Julie doesn't mind whether anybody else likes it – she admires it every day. She didn't buy it because of any advertising campaign. If the neighbours change their furniture, Julie isn't going to change ours. She says to me, "It is so beautiful. I am uplifted just looking at it." Most importantly, if Julie ever had to sell it, she wouldn't feel a lesser person without it.

It is likely that you have a bunch of books, gadgets, photographs, souvenirs, or maybe a car or a boat that you treasure. That's wonderful – and no doubt they make your life more pleasurable and more convenient. It is *personal appreciation*. It has nothing to do with what anybody else thinks or whether anyone else is impressed.

In a Nutshell
You will be happy *with* stuff only if you can be happy *without* stuff.

Excuse No. 6: *I'll be happy when...*

My 75 kilo neighbour proclaimed, "I'm going on a diet. I'll be happy when I'm 60 kilos." So she postponed her happiness for five months – and when she hit 61 kilos, her boyfriend left the country. Now she is 60 kilos but she can't be happy unless Bobby comes back.

How often do we postpone happiness?

We see happiness as some kind of distant mirage – as if we are crawling through the desert and there's a sign ahead which says "HAPPINESS," and we say, "If I can just make it THERE, then I'll be happy." We have it logically figured out, "We can't be happy yet because we're still paying for the car. But next April..." And next April comes and the kids have the flu, the in-laws are coming to stay, and we say, "Around next October..."

Life is never sorted out! You eventually graduate with your degree. You start your dream job only to find your boss has body odour. You finally take a family vacation and your father falls and breaks his leg. You say, "Once I get this divorce, I'll make a fresh start. My life won't be so complicated." Your life is always going to be complicated.

Now, you can minimise the complications, but you won't eliminate them! So you have to enjoy yourself while you're in the middle of it. Be fascinated. If you're being taken to court, if you are having surgery, be entertained. Enjoy the ride.

I'll be happy when there's world peace

Mary says, "I'll never be happy until there is world peace." That may seem noble, but it's not very intelligent! Better to be happy in the meantime – and work at making your little corner of the world more peaceful. It is possible to accept the world as it is and still accept a share of responsibility to improve things.

In a Nutshell
The happiest people aren't waiting for anything to happen.

2

Conquering Crises

Negative thoughts are like rats. They arrive in groups. One shows up and before you know it they have taken over.

Example: You take a phone call from a rude customer at work. Your first thought is, *"I hate rude people."*

Followed by your next negative thought, "In this job *I'm surrounded by rude people!"*

And your next negative thought, "In this job I'm surrounded by rude people *and I'm underpaid."*

And the next, "In this job I'm surrounded by rude people and I'm underpaid *and underappreciated."*

And then, "In this job I'm surrounded by rude people and I'm underpaid and underappreciated *and come to think of it I'm not appreciated at home either."*

Now the rats are arriving in droves: "In this job I'm surrounded by rude people and I'm underpaid and underappreciated and come to think of it I'm not appreciated at home either *and tonight I'll have to cook dinner, why can't my useless husband get off his*

ANDREW MATTHEWS

backside, my mother always told me I was making a serious mistake... and now I've got a headache, maybe it's a tumour!"

Is this scenario familiar? A lone rat becomes a plague.

You need an extermination strategy and here is the best approach I know to rid yourself of the rats. The moment you have your first negative thought, ask yourself, "What's good about this?"

What's good about confronting rude people?

- I'm building character and patience.
- I'm developing people skills that will help me in my next job.
- The rude people at work help me to appreciate my husband.

Now you might say, "Let's be realistic." HERE'S REALISTIC:

- Lousy things happen.
- You have to make the best of things.
- Happy people have the habit of saying, "What's good about this?"
- Do you want to be happy or not?

You break your leg – "What's good about this?"

- I get to rest.
- I learn to empathise with sick people.
- I get to read some great books.
- I can't vacuum for a month.

Your girlfriend dumps you – "What's good about this?"

- I can save money.
- I can watch all the football I like.
- I can be less hygienic.
- No need to vacuum at all!

In a Nutshell

One negative thought attracts another.

One positive thought attracts another.

Before the plague starts, ask yourself, "What's good about this?"

It's Not What Happens To You...

It's not WHAT HAPPENS TO YOU that matters most. It's how YOU FEEL ABOUT what happens to you.

EXAMPLE: Let's say that you are at the airport, waiting to catch a flight, and the airline tells you,

"Sorry! Mechanical trouble. You won't be leaving for three hours!" You get very angry. You tell yourself, "This is terrible! I'll miss the sales meeting. What a disaster!" While you remain stressed, things will get worse! People will trip over you, spill coffee in your lap and lose your baggage. When you fight life, life always wins!

BA 375 TOKYO DELAYED

Then finally you cool down. You tell yourself, "There's nothing I can do about it. I am probably where I am meant to be. I'll make the most of it."

Suddenly, everything changes! From nowhere an old friend appears, or you make a new friend, or you stumble on a fresh opportunity – and life begins to support you. Once we change our thoughts about "a bad situation," we can take advantage of it. Life's great opportunities mostly arrive disguised as misfortune and disaster.

EXAMPLE: Imagine two women, Mary and Jane. Both get divorced.

Mary says, "I've failed. My life is over."

Jane says, "My life has just begun!"

Who will blossom?

In a Nutshell

Every "disaster" in your life is not so much a disaster, as a situation waiting for you to change your mind about it.

Alison's Story

At 27 I had a job in the corporate world with dreams of marriage, children and a happy life. Then in December 1994 while parking my car outside my home in Port Elizabeth, South Africa, I was abducted by two strange men. They drove me to remote bushland. They raped me and strangled me. As I lay there unconscious, they stabbed me in the lower stomach more than 30 times. They cut my throat from ear to ear. Then they left me naked, to die.

I remember thinking, "If I am to die here, let me make one last effort to bring these monsters to justice." From their conversation I knew their first names. I scratched their names in the sand with my finger.

I was 80 metres from the road but if I was to have any chance of survival, I somehow had to get there.

When your throat has been cut from ear to ear, you have no muscles to hold your head forward. So when I stood up, my head flipped over and rested on my back. My insides were also spilling out. So using one hand to hold my head in place and the other hand to keep my stomach together, I half crawled, half staggered toward the road.

It was now after 2 a.m. and I knew that so far from town there would be few passing cars. I lay bleeding in the centre of the road until eventually a vehicle approached. The engine slowed, the car stopped but no one got out. The headlights shone right onto me. Surely the occupants of the car could see me? I waved frantically. A long time passed – it felt like 10 to 15 minutes. Still no one got out. I heard the engine rev and then suddenly the car manoeuvred itself around my body and sped off. It was a Volkswagen Beetle and I watched the tail-lights become pinpricks in the distance. I could feel myself slipping away.

A Glimmer of Hope
Sometime later I sensed a second set of headlights.

This time the car stopped. There were voices. Someone called an ambulance. As I found out later, one of the passengers was a veterinary student named Tiaan. Tiaan checked my pulse and my tongue. Immediately he understood that if I lost consciousness, I would die. He covered me with his shirt, he held my hand and began to talk to me.

When your throat is cut, you can breathe but you can't speak. Tiaan continued to ask me questions, encouraging me to answer with a squeeze of my hand – one squeeze for *yes*, two for *no*. He kept telling me, "You have beautiful green eyes. Open your eyes. Let me see your beautiful eyes." So I did my best to keep my eyes open, and tried to keep squeezing his hand until the ambulance arrived.

I was rushed to the Provincial Hospital for emergency surgery. My trachea, larynx and thyroid had been slashed, the major muscles and veins in my neck were severed and my intestines were lacerated. I was on the operating table for three hours. Somehow the medical team sewed me back together. Days later I was given a hand mirror. To my surprise I saw that the whites of my eyes were completely red, like pieces of raw beefsteak. My first thought was, "I look terrible – but how did my eyes look when I was bleeding to death on the road?" I had to find out! I asked the nurses, "Were my eyes like this when the ambulance brought me in?"

They explained, "When those guys strangled you,

it burst every capillary in your eyeballs." I felt such a mix of gratitude and embarrassment – gratitude to Tiaan that he would do whatever it took to keep me conscious – and embarrassment that I looked so terrible every time I showed him my "beautiful" eyes!

I had been disembowelled and my throat was slashed 16 times. I should never have survived. But even amidst the brutality and horror, I was lucky:

- If not for Tiaan I would have died on that road.
- There were only two thoracic surgeons stationed in the whole of Port Elizabeth – and one of them happened to be on duty when I arrived at the Provincial Hospital at 4 a.m.
- The doctors explained that when my abductors strangled me, they crushed my windpipe. I was suffocating. I asked, "What saved me?"

The doctors said, "Luckily, they cut your throat and opened your airway!"

For the next few months, I was in pain – excruciating, mindblowing pain – but I gradually recovered. There was a very public trial at which I gave evidence. My assailants were sentenced to life imprisonment.

Nothing Left

I had survived the attack and then the court appearances, and it was time to get on with my life. But when the worst was over, I had nothing left. I went into deep depression. It took me months to find a reason to get out of bed. My mother remained my strength and my rock. From the moment she arrived at my hospital bedside and throughout the trial I never saw her shed a tear. It was only later I discovered how often she wept alone.

> "They raped me and strangled me... They cut my throat from ear to ear."

I told myself, "You didn't fight so hard to survive – and then do nothing with your life." People began to ask me to share my story at meetings and conferences. I feared public speaking but I did want to somehow make a difference – and so I began the work I do now.

I have forgiven my attackers. I did it for myself. I refuse to carry hate and resentment for the rest of my life. I pity them. They are in the past.

I married in 1997 and the greatest miracle of all – despite the horrific wounds to my entire reproductive area – I have given birth to two beautiful children.

I tell the whole story in my book, *I Have Life*. Today I get to speak all over the world. And my message? *Life is beautiful. Life is worth fighting for. It's not what happens to you, it's what you do with it.*

Alison's website: www.alison.co.za

Flexibility

Here's a recipe for permanent misery...

a) Decide how you think the world SHOULD be.

b) Make rules for how everyone SHOULD behave. Then, when the world doesn't obey your rules, *get angry!* That's what miserable people do!

Let's say you expect that:

- friends SHOULD return favours
- people SHOULD appreciate you
- planes SHOULD arrive on time
- everyone SHOULD be honest
- your husband SHOULD remember your birthday.

These expectations may sound reasonable. But often, these things won't happen! So you end up frustrated and disappointed.

There's a better strategy. Make fewer demands. Instead, have preferences! For things that are beyond your control, tell yourself, "I WOULD PREFER 'A,' BUT IF 'B' HAPPENS, IT'S OK TOO!" This is really a game that you play in your head. But if you make the game a habit, you have more peace of mind... You prefer that people are polite, but when they are rude, it doesn't ruin your day. You prefer sunshine, but rain is okay! In other words, you are flexible.

Another thought: if you notice that your own blunders and disasters sometimes turn into glorious opportunities, wouldn't that be so for the rest of humanity? So you may have a sister who *eats too much* or a husband who *drinks too much* or a colleague who *gets the sack*. And while you are agonising over their life journeys, they are benefiting from their own blunders and disasters.

If only the world were a better place...

We might point to the starving in Calcutta as if to say, "Everything is going wrong." That can be an excuse for not making our own lives work. If you are an Indian, or if you're living in Calcutta and helping the Indians, perhaps the situation makes a little more sense. But to judge situations we don't fully understand from a distance isn't helpful. If you want to make a difference, and do something about it, that's another matter. But agonising doesn't help. The Mother Teresas of the world don't agonise – they act.

Fred says, "If only there wasn't so much wrong with the world, I could be happy." Well, Fred this is the only world you have got. You may as well be happy with it. The world is likely much better than you believe. But we get a distorted picture of the world we live in.

Imagine that you spotted these front page headlines at a newspaper stand: *145 Countries Not At War This Week, 7000 Banks Not Robbed Yesterday, No Threat of Bird Flu, Dog Flu, Mouse Flu or Moose Flu This Year!* and this: *98% of Parents are Very Nice to Their Children...*

Would you say to yourself, "Amazing! I need to buy that paper right now!" You wouldn't! Or imagine you were a marketing executive for Toyota or Coca-Cola, and I came to your office to sell you a double-page spread in that same paper, with those same stories. What would you say? "You've got rocks in your head. No one will read that!"

When it comes to news, people get excited and curious about threats, danger and absurdity. We like to

be scared and surprised. So newspapers, radio and TV scare, excite and surprise us. I'm not saying it's good or bad – it's just how it is. With some exceptions, things of beauty and acts of kindness and generosity don't make the headlines. A thousand husbands surprise their wives with flowers and one brings home a knife. Which guy gets famous? The world you live in is more beautiful and more uplifting than the world you see in the news. It always will be.

Embracing Change

The seasons come and go, inflation goes up and down, people get hired and fired. You'd think we'd learn that the underlying law of the universe is change! Instead we get angry. We return to our favourite vacation spot after five years, and we groan, "It's not the same." Bread goes up 30p, and we get upset. We say to our lover, "It's not like when I met you" – whatever that means.

People seek enlightenment. But the measure of our enlightenment is not whether we meditate at dawn or eat bean sprouts for breakfast. The measure of our wisdom is much more about whether we embrace changing circumstances and accept people who are different from ourselves.

In a Nutshell
Happy people welcome change. They're the guys who say, "Why would I even want my next five years to be like my last five?"

When Life Hurts

When you accidentally bite your tongue, it's hard to see "pain" as something positive. The same goes for a blister on your big toe – who needs a throbbing foot? But what if you felt no pain? How often would you bite off bits of your tongue – or burn your backside in the bath?

Physical pain is a marvellous alarm system that prevents further damage. It tells us, "You'd better change what you're doing!" Emotional pain gives us a similar message, i.e. "You'd better change how you're thinking!" It's normal to get angry or jealous or a bit resentful – temporarily. But if those feelings become permanent the message may be:

- Don't expect to control other people.
- Don't expect other people to behave like you.
- Don't depend on other people to make you happy!

While we keep thinking the same thoughts, we keep

feeling the same pain. And then we say, "But I'm right!" Unfortunately being "right" doesn't help!

A blister on our foot is a message to change our shoes. With emotional pain – which feels like a blister on the brain – the message is usually to change our thinking. Our egos love to be right. So we sometimes hang on to anger, blame and resentment for years – "I may be miserable but I'm *right!*"

The good thing about pain and suffering is that they erode the ego. When we can no longer stand the pain, we shift from "I'm right – there is no other way to see this!" to "I can't take it anymore – maybe I could have a different point of view!"

Recall an incident in the last week that disturbed you: you were abused in traffic, your boyfriend called you "Fatty," your wallet was stolen. Realise it wasn't the incident that was disturbing, it was your thoughts about it. You say, "*Anybody* would have been upset." Wrong. *Most* people.

All our lives we've been conditioned to think certain thoughts about things. It's the thoughts that make us unhappy – and we can change our thoughts.

In a Nutshell
With both physical and emotional pain, when we keep doing the same thing, it keeps hurting!

Is it True?
It is not the situation, it is our thoughts about a situation.

We can learn from people who have come back from the depths of despair.

Byron Katie was a self-employed businesswoman and mother of three. She was depressed and suicidal for ten years. She hated herself so much that she would spend weeks without getting out of bed, taking a bath or brushing her teeth. Her self-esteem plunged so low that she even stopped sleeping in her bed, preferring to punish herself by sleeping on the floor.

It was while lying on the floor watching a cockroach crawl up her leg that she had a kind of awakening. (Don't try this at home!) She realised that none of her pain was caused by *her situation*. Her suffering was caused by *her thoughts about her situation*. And the problem wasn't even that she *had* the thoughts, but that she *believed* the thoughts. In other words:

- It's not the world that makes us unhappy.
- It's not even our thoughts about the world that make us unhappy.
- It's when we believe our thoughts about the world that we become unhappy.

You say, "Buddha could have told Katie that!" Correct, but sometimes we need to suffer before we get the message. "Katie," as she is known, felt inspired to write down four questions that we can ask ourselves when we are deeply troubled:

- Is the thought true?
- Can you absolutely know the thought is true?
- How do you react when you believe that thought?
- Who would you be without that thought?

These questions became the foundation of her books and workshops. They are useful tools for investigating the real cause of our suffering. How would this work?

Example 1:

Katie tells the story of a woman – we'll call her Jane. Jane's husband had an affair with the next-door neighbour. For Jane it was a living nightmare. Every day she watched him come home and fall into the woman's arms. She saw them cuddling on the porch. Angry and resentful, Jane began to neglect her life and her children.

Jane told herself, *"All I want is for my husband to come home to me."* Then after months of self-torture she came across the four questions. She asked herself,

- Can I know it is absolutely true?
- Do I really want my husband to come back?

Her mind opened just for a moment and she realised that it might not be true. She realised that perhaps she didn't want to live with her husband anymore. She also discovered that *it wasn't her husband* that was upsetting her – it was her *thoughts* about her husband. She flipped the thought, "I want him to come home to me," and asked herself, "Do I want *me* to come home to me." In other words, "Is it up to *me* to start caring for myself?"

Jane stopped wishing for her husband to do *anything*. She began to nurture herself and her children. Her whole life changed. She discovered that she was actually very happy for the neighbour to take care of her husband! She even began to feel gratitude to the woman next door!

Now, you might say, "If my husband moved in with the woman next door, I would find happiness by having his legs broken!" But here's the point: when you argue with reality, reality always wins. It doesn't matter how resentful you get or how many times you say, "It shouldn't have happened!" What *is*, is.

Be prepared to question your thinking, "Are my thoughts true or am I making assumptions?" Katie's questions help us to distinguish between facts and opinions. Accept the facts, question the opinions:

- "My husband is having an affair" – that is fact.
- "I can't be happy without my husband" – that is opinion.

In a Nutshell
Facts are *what is*.
The first step to happiness is accepting *what is*.

Example 2:
Your son has an accident. His car collides with a truck, removing the entire roof of his vehicle. He is badly brain-injured, he slips into a coma and doctors don't expect him to survive the night. Ultimately he lives but at a huge cost. His right side is paralysed, he is partially blinded, he is unable to speak, and he has short-term memory loss. He is unable to study or work.

Why this example?

This is the story of my stepson, Michael – Julie's son. Michael hit the truck in November 1986. It would have been easy to believe, "Michael can't be happy because he will never be normal. We can't be happy because Michael will never be like he was."

But did we absolutely know that was true?

- A lot of perfectly healthy people are unhappy.
- A lot of brain-injured people are happier than most.
- Families faced with huge challenges are often the happiest and the most loving.

Julie said, "What we have is what we have. We'll live one day at a time." Watching Julie these last 20 years, I begin to appreciate the depth of a mother's love. I remain in awe of her courage and her resilience. Michael's positive attitude became an example for all of us.

We have found a way to be happy. It hasn't always been easy.

In a Nutshell
Next time you want to tell yourself, "I can't be happy because..." ask yourself, "Do I know that this is absolutely true?"

Can You Choose Happiness?

I grew up assuming that your happiness depended on what happened to you. I figured, "When I have fewer problems, I'll be happy!" Then gradually I realised that the happiest people I knew had more problems than I did!

Maybe you have noticed the same thing – those people who get the most out of life have often had it tough. They have lost loved ones, they've gone broke, they've been dumped, sacked or suffered serious illness – and most likely, they still have big problems! But they are happy because at some point they decided "happy" is the only way to live. Happiness doesn't just happen to you, like some "accident."

Twenty-five years ago I had a neighbour, Caroline. Caroline seemed happier than anyone I knew. Caroline genuinely appreciated people – she enjoyed everybody, no matter who they were or what they did.

She would say to me, "You have to meet Ross. He's wonderful! You'll love him." Or she would tell me, "Come and meet Sharyn – she is one of my dearest friends. She's amazing." So I would meet Ross the waiter or Playstead the pilot or Joe the gardener or Nabil the ex-terrorist, and I would think, "Well, they're nice – but they're not amazing!" I certainly didn't fall in love with them.

But Caroline just loved them – sincerely loved them. And she was constantly cheerful. When I met her she had just lost her mother to cancer and her husband had run off with an older woman. But still she looked on the bright side.

Caroline drove a little white Mini Minor – and one day while she was driving home from work it caught fire. The car was wrecked. I bumped into her that evening and she told me with an enormous smile, "Guess what – my car caught fire!"

You would have thought she had won the lottery! I could resist no longer. I said, "Caroline, why are you always so damned happy?" She laughed, "I *decided* to be. I got tired of being miserable!"

I figured Caroline was either joking or crazy. The idea that you might actually *choose* happiness seemed strangely ridiculous. I thought that happiness was like influenza – sometimes you get it, sometimes you don't. Could you choose to be happy?

A month later Caroline did win the lottery – and the prize was a brand new car. Of course, she was happy – but no happier than when the Mini Minor caught fire.

Do you really want to be happy?

A lot of people will tell you, "I really want to be happy!" But what do they think about? What do they talk about? What do they dwell on?

When you *really* want to be happy, you quit complaining about your arthritis. When you *really* want to be happy, you quit resenting your boyfriend. Maybe you leave him, maybe you don't, but either way, you throw out your mental list of all his faults.

If you really want to be happy, you will be.

We become addicted to misery and complaining. Mary says, "Well, this happened so I have to talk about it." No you don't, Mary! You don't have to eat everything you see and you don't have to talk about everything that happens.

Some people say they want to be happy, but it is not an intense burning desire. It is more like, "I want to be happy *if I don't have to change how I think.*" That's not a big enough commitment. When we have suffered enough, then we get serious. We decide, "I can't take it anymore, I want to be happy."

This might come as a shock: if you aren't happy now, maybe you haven't wanted it enough.

When you really, really want to be happy, here is what will happen:
  • you will think about things that make you feel good
  • you will talk about things that make you feel good.

Here's a simple exercise: every morning when you open your eyes, decide to be happy – not for forever, just today. Tell yourself, "Today I want to be happy." In the shower, tell yourself, "I want to be happy." When the neighbours are screaming, when some idiot cuts you off on the freeway, tell yourself, "I want to be happy." When everything seems to be going wrong, and when everything seems to be going right, tell yourself, "I want to be happy." You become what you think about.

Geoff's Story

As the paramedics carried me out of the house one of them asked Jillian quietly, "Where would your husband prefer to die?"

Four months ago I was a breath away from death. Now, the cancer "markings" in my blood that spiralled to 22,000 at their worst are down to 170.

A miracle? Well, it will do me. In fact, two doctors – my oncologist and my intensive care specialist – both dubbed me "Lazarus," neither knowing the other had done so. That's how close it was.

It began on 2 August 2007 when, after three months of complaining to my GP of needing to get up in the middle of the night to pee, I was sent to a specialist. The scans were bad. The biopsy was worse. I was diagnosed with bladder cancer – and our lives were turned upside down in an instant. My wife Jillian had endured her own battle with breast cancer years before. Now she had to tell our 22-year-old daughter Madeline and 16-year-old son Sam the bad news.

Happy Birthday!
So for my 57th birthday – 13 August – I had a six-hour operation. I learned that while some of the cancer had been removed along with my bladder, I would need

ongoing treatment including chemotherapy.

After months of treatment I was starting to feel I had it beaten, but then the cancer returned, this time wrapping itself around the outside of my rectum. Result: more chemo and 33 sessions of radiotherapy, five days a week. Next came a bowel blockage that also turned out to be cancer.

> "If I was dying, the timing was lousy."

Last December, the four of us arrived in London to start a six-week trip to England, Europe and the United States. Immediately, I felt so ill I couldn't eat. My stomach ballooned. I checked into St Thomas' Hospital in Westminster.

If I was dying, the timing was lousy. This particular day after my arrival was set up for a reunion with five mates from my Fleet Street days working at the *Daily Express* in the 1970s. But there would be no reunion. In fact, no holiday. The English doctors said that the cancer was inoperable and that I should return to Australia immediately and go into palliative care. I had only months or weeks to live, they said.

Merry Christmas!

It gets worse. Because of the severity of my condition, according to airline rules, I could not make the 24-hour trip home without a qualified medical practitioner accompanying me. Christmas Day was just three days away. Where would we find someone to make a return trip to Australia at such a time?

I had given up believing in Father Christmas half a century ago, but I now believe in him again. And this one is real. The first person my wife Jillian thought to ask for advice was a surgeon friend, Bernie. He was having Christmas drinks when Jillian called. When she asked if he knew of anyone who might make a mercy dash to England, he didn't flinch.

"I will be on the next plane," he said. Jillian was gobsmacked that he would give up Christmas with his family to bring me home. Within hours, Bernie was on his way. After just six hours in London (and a quick Christmas lunch with my family but no sleep), he was briefed about my condition, loaded up with the necessary medical equipment and instructions on what to do if anything went wrong. On arrival in Melbourne, an ambulance whisked me straight to Epworth Hospital.

Despite the English doctors' gloomy prognosis, I wasn't going to palliative care. My doctor wouldn't hear of it.

All of that was seven months ago. Today I am back to 85 kilos – 23 more than when I was so thin and weak that most people assumed my days were numbered. My doctors admitted my prospects were grim, but never gave up on me. Within 24 hours of my return, they performed emergency bowel surgery and organised new chemo treatment.

Things Get Worse
But soon things got worse before they got better. Days

after starting the new treatment in January I awoke feeling so weak I told Jillian, "I think I'm going to die." I was nearly right. Without the two paramedics who were at my bedside within four minutes of my son making a 000 call, and the brilliance of the Epworth emergency department, I almost certainly would not have survived.

They decided I probably had an infection from my latest chemo treatment and needed antibiotics. Fast. Septicaemia had set in and without antibiotics I would die, and they knew it. As the paramedics carried me out of the house one of them asked Jillian quietly, "Where would your husband prefer to die?" and she said, "At home." Instead, that night I was perched up in bed in intensive care, eating sandwiches and drinking coffee. Better still, next day I got encouraging news from my doctor: "If the new chemo you are being treated with almost killed you," he told me, "there's a good chance it could be killing your cancer as well."

He was right. I was soon to discover the chemotherapy worked a treat.

Not only have those cancer marker levels hit rock bottom, but I am back walking normally, my legs have muscles again and my appetite and yearning for a glass of chardonnay (which had vanished for months) have returned.

A few months ago Jillian would add ice cream, force-feed me chocolate bars, anything to put some weight on me. Times change. This week she scolded me for eating too many biscuits. I didn't know whether to laugh or cry.

It has been an unbelievable and, at times, heartbreaking journey. Cancer is like that. But it can be beaten. Not that I have beaten it completely – my doctors insist they will never guarantee I'm cured – but thanks to wonderful medics and the support of my family who have pushed and pulled me through it all, I'm still here.

3

Thoughts

Your Mind is a Magnet

Your thoughts are magnetic. When you are feeling good, you attract uplifting experiences and when you are feeling bad...

Last month I was sitting on a plane waiting to depart from Hobart airport. I was pondering how best to explain the law of attraction... How do I illustrate by example that we attract people and circumstances consistent with how we feel... *that when we feel happy, we attract positive circumstances and when we feel upset and angry, we attract events to make us feel worse?*

The plane was slightly delayed by a final rather breathless and angry-looking passenger. When she saw that someone had parked a large briefcase in the spot above *her seat,* she became more angry. When she discovered that there was no room for her bags *anywhere* in the overhead locker, she began to look seriously disturbed.

And so she sat seething for the entire flight with her baggage wedged between her feet. You might guess the story from here... We landed, the owner of the briefcase stood up, reached over to retrieve it from the locker – and dropped it on her head!

Bam! When you think that life is against you, it is.

When you are happy, life and people reward you in the most unexpected ways. When you are stressed, angry, and feeling like a victim, life kicks you in the teeth. When you leave the office feeling irate, people abuse you in the subway. The reverse is also true. How different the world looks when we fall in love!

The world is a mirror – what you feel inside, you get on the outside – which is why YOU CAN'T FIX LIFE BY WORKING ON THE OUTSIDE. If people on the street are unfriendly, changing streets doesn't help! If nobody at work gives you any respect, changing jobs won't fix it.

Most of us learned things inside out! We learned, "If you don't like your job, change it. If you don't like your wife, change her." Sometimes it's appropriate to change your job or your partner. But if you don't change your thinking, you are setting yourself up for more of the same.

Can we explain this scientifically?

At school, your teachers showed you neat models of atoms and told you, "Atoms are the building blocks of everything." You learned that an atom consists of some tiny balls of solid stuff orbiting through space. This idea of a few solid balls of stuff circling through empty space is a very convenient model of atoms – but very inconveniently, it's wrong! The material world seems solid – but it is not.

Quantum physics, which is the study of *sub-atomic matter*, has long since established these "solid bits of stuff" are in fact collections of *energy*. Nothing that we think is solid is really *solid*. THE UNIVERSE IS NOT LIKE A BIG MACHINE – BUT MUCH MORE LIKE A BIG THOUGHT.

The new-age idea that everything is *consciousness* is actually cutting-edge science!

Every *thought* and every *thing* has its own unique vibration. Vibration is the language of the universe and with every thought you think, you are communicating with the universe. This is probably no revelation to you. You know it and you have experienced the effects.

You say, "Okay, so everything is made of thought energy – including my Toyota, my mother-in-law and this book I'm reading right now. But my thoughts are just one small collection of energy in this massive universe. How could *my thoughts* possibly attract things and create circumstances?"

Look at it this way: imagine that you were to take a trip inside your liver. You would see millions of tiny cells: growing, dividing, dying. But it would look very random and chaotic. Nothing would make sense.

Looking at your whole liver, it would make *more sense*. But only in the context of your *entire body* would the whole thing become magical – you'd see billions of cells cooperating in ways we will never fully understand.

So it is with our thoughts. With our thoughts we are *connected to everything* in ways we don't understand.

But that is so improbable!

Fred says, "But that is just too fantastic to believe!" Of course it is too fantastic! The universe itself is BOTH improbable and too fantastic.

For example: the universe is expanding at the speed of light. Is that fantastic? And what is at the edge of this expanding universe – a fence?

One cell in your toenail or bladder contains the blueprint for your entire body. Is that fantastic? What about life itself – and how you grew from a single fertilised cell to be reading this book. Is that fantastic? It is all miraculous.

Julie's Accident

One morning in September 2004, Julie and I had a disagreement. I said something insensitive that made her seriously angry. I have no idea what I said but no doubt Julie remembers! In 20 years I had never seen her so mad. As she grabbed her car keys and left for her appointment, I thought to myself, "No one who is as irate as Julie is right now should be anywhere near an automobile!"

Not ten minutes later, she was sitting in her car at an intersection, perfectly stationary. A van approached the crossroads at high speed, lost control – and drove straight into Julie's car. Thank God, she escaped unhurt.

As Julie soon discovered, the van was driven by another very angry lady. You ask:

- Was Julie thinking about a car accident? No!
- Did Julie want the accident? No!
- Was she experiencing intense negative emotion? Yes.
- Did she have an intensely negative experience to match? Absolutely!

You say, "But Julie's car wasn't even moving. It wasn't

her fault!" Ask Julie and she will admit that she created her experience. She will tell you that she had a head full of "today is lousy" thoughts. And life delivered a lousy experience. You are a magnet. How you feel about yourself determines the quality of your experience.

You say, "Does that mean that everyone who is angry in a car will have an accident?" No. It means that if you are full of an energy that says "life stinks," then life will deliver you "life stinks" experiences. And if you are driving a car at the time, an accident is more likely.

> **In a Nutshell**
> Uplifting thoughts attract uplifting experiences.
> Angry, victim-type thoughts attract low energy
> experiences.

We Attract What We Feel

How often have you found yourself in precisely the situation that you didn't want? You said to yourself, "If there is one thing I don't want to happen... if there is one question I don't want to be asked... if there is one mistake that I don't want to repeat..." and what did you get?

You get divorced. You go out on your first dinner date. You say, "If there is one person I don't want to see it's my stupid ex-husband." Who shows up at the next table?

We attract what we fear. The Bible says, "Resist not evil." It means don't focus on bad stuff. It means *don't spend your life thinking about illness and car crashes and your ex-husband* – fill your mind with thoughts of health and happiness.

We attract what we feel. While you feel unloved you cannot attract love. While you feel lonely you cannot attract friends. While you feel broke you cannot attract prosperity.

When life is tough, we are part of the problem. You say, "But when my life gets better I will feel better." There's the catch. YOU NEED TO FEEL BETTER FIRST – about yourself, about your work, about your bank balance – then things get better.

Patterns

Fred says, "Wait a minute! If your thoughts create your circumstances, then people who have lots of victim thoughts would keep getting the same old crap! There would be people who always get sick, people who always get into fights and people who keep dating losers."

He argues, "If your thoughts create your life, then you would have people with *rich thoughts* who keep getting richer and people with *poor thoughts* who keep getting poorer!" Fred says, "If your thoughts create your life, there would be happy people who sail from one adventure to another and miserable people who stagger from one disaster to another!"

Right. That is how it is. That is how it has always been.

Some people are always broke! You can hand them

£5,000 cash and before you know it they need a bank loan to buy a pizza.

Some of us are always busy – and will find any excuse not to relax.

Some people are forever getting ripped off – by salesmen, phone companies, old girlfriends and long lost relatives.

Did you ever meet a lady who said, "I always end up dating jerks"? She has a radar for finding rude, selfish, lazy people – and then dates them!

Some people are always late! They can get up at six to be at work by nine, and at 10:15 they are still combing the house for car keys.

Some guys keep getting into fistfights. Years ago I had a friend called John, and one night he invited me to go out for a drink. We had been at a bar for about 20 minutes when I noticed there was a fight happening in the corner. Some guy was being strangled – and on closer investigation, I noticed it was John.

I went over and politely asked the large hairy truck driver who was choking John to let him go. John and I went to another bar. He ordered a drink and I went to the men's room. On returning I saw a crowd of people around the pool table thumping somebody. It was John!

As I dragged him out to the car, he proceeded to tell me about another exciting nightspot we should visit. He explained about the fights. He said, "It's unavoidable!" John is typical of people who experience history repeating itself. They tell you, "There's nothing I can do," arguing either:

a) "it's how the world is," or

b) "it's just the way I am – and I can't change."

Neither of these statements is true.

Of course, we also have good patterns. Some people make friends wherever they go. Some people make money wherever they go. Some people have fun wherever they go. Some footballers are always where the ball is.

Some people always land on their feet – their pattern says *things always work out...* Dave's car breaks down in the middle of nowhere and a stranger picks him up, drives him home and then offers him a job. You think it is coincidence?

Why Did This Happen to Me?

We have these subconscious behaviour patterns – automatic programs – but the patterns are not "us." For example, there is a way you handle money that is automatic – requires no thinking. There's a way you handle people or problems that is automatic. There's a way you might keep yourself busy that is automatic. There's a way you make yourself late that requires no thinking.

When we keep having the same thoughts we keep reinforcing the same self-image and the same behaviour. When we keep having the same thoughts we keep attracting similar circumstances, similar people and similar outcomes.

In a Nutshell
Fred says, "I think like I do because my life is a mess!" No Fred, your life is a mess because you think like you do!

Is thought more important than action?
Both matter. Action is thought in motion. Action accelerates results. When you take action you demonstrate your belief.

67

For example:

- You save money every week – you confirm your belief that a debt-free life is possible.
- You make a sales call – you confirm your belief that a sale is possible.
- You lift weights – you confirm your belief that fitness is possible.

Action is part of the process – you need to do more than just *visualise* prosperity or a healthy body. But if you take lots of action but never hold in your mind what you want to achieve, you'll work very hard for limited returns.

Your Daily Habit

Here is an exercise used by millions. Every morning, before you are assaulted by the morning news, close your eyes and imagine your day ahead. Visualise your day as perfect. See yourself happy, efficient, confident, loving, and healthy. See your day unfolding as you want. See yourself energetic and relaxed, laughing, enjoying your family and friends, comfortable with who you are, conquering challenges, always in the right place at the right time.

Make your own news!

Will your day be perfect? It will be much *better than if you hadn't done it.* And when you do the same exercise tomorrow and the next day and the next, your life will more and more closely reflect what you picture each morning. Make a list of what you want in your life and pin it on your wall. Review it before your morning visualisation.

I know of no more powerful daily discipline than this. It is deceptively simple. The most useful disciplines always are. If there are five words that should be ingrained into the mind of every school child they are *focus on what you want.*

Rod's Story

It should have been a time of celebration, one of the happiest days of my life…

It was 1998. I was married with three beautiful children: they were three, four and eight years old. My wife and I were being flown to Wellington where I was to receive an award for coming 9th out of 150 salesmen.

It was in the car, driving to the airport that she told me, "I've had enough of you. I want a divorce." My heart sank. I couldn't believe it. I felt weak and confused. I didn't want my wife to leave me. All I could think of was my dear children: too young and vulnerable to come from a broken home. Shattered, I cried my eyes out all the way to Wellington.

Mine is a common story:

- *I had a goal for our family*: to earn heaps of money, own a nice home, educate the kids and travel.
- *I had no idea:* my wife was in love with my best mate and it had all been happening under my nose.
- *They had a plan:* the day I moved out of my family home, he moved in. It tore my guts out.

- *I should have listened to my intuition years ago: deep down, I always sensed it could end like this. I could have walked away before we got committed.*

Overnight I lost my wife, my kids, my home and my friend. Over the next 12 months I lost my business, all my money, my drive and my faith in the legal system. Our family home was sold just before the bank foreclosed. I lost my faith in people. I lost everything.

> "As a dad, it seemed like everything was stacked against me."

As a dad, it seemed like everything was stacked against me. I saw my children once a week, on Sundays for an hour. I missed them terribly – every night I cried myself to sleep. Meanwhile, I was painted as the bad guy. As I found out later, the kids were being manipulated and mentally abused.

It's tough to stay positive when you are on your own. I read motivational books, I used affirmations and went to counselling. I also watched *The Secret* video which invigorated me and led me into meditation. I read Andrew Matthews' books. Everything helped.

I kept loving my kids and I kept fighting in the courts. One year and thousands of dollars later the courts saw sense, and I won custody of my children. Eleven years later I have a lovely partner and happy kids. I love my work – I am a financial coach – and I have rebuilt my business. I feel fortunate and successful. Sure, I lost my children for a year, I went through buckets of pain and heartache, but I wouldn't change anything.

Life can be hard. Never quit! If you want something bad enough, no matter what the odds, you can do it. Today I am a proud and happy man.

Rod's website: www.brackenridge.biz

4

Like Yourself!

Winners And Losers

In 1958 a New Yorker by the name of Robert Lane had a son. Robert already had several children and perhaps he was running out of ideas for names – so he called the new baby "Winner."

Three years later Robert had another son – and he decided to call him... what do you think? "Loser!" So now there are two brothers, a *Winner* and a *Loser*. The boys grew up. One child won a scholarship to college, graduated and joined the New York Police Department. One child went to jail.

Who do you think went to university and who went to jail?

Loser graduated from Lafayette College and joined the NYPD. His buddies on the beat call him Lou. Winner has been arrested nearly three dozen times for burglary, trespassing and domestic violence.

Most of us would think that when your Dad calls you *Loser*, it's an unlucky break. But it's not what other people think about you, it's *how you see yourself that matters* – even if you start out life as a loser.

As Within, So Without

Years ago I noticed that whenever I was having a bad day, or whenever I felt angry, that was the day I would accidentally cut my foot, bang my head or burn my backside. It was on those days when I didn't like myself or when I was telling myself "I'm a hopeless idiot" that I would manage to punish myself. I also discovered that when I felt good about myself, other people were more friendly.

Have you noticed that when you are feeling good, other people become very nice? Isn't it funny how they change? The world is a reflection of us. When we dislike ourselves, we dislike everybody else. When we love being who we are, the rest of the world is wonderful.

Our self-image is the blueprint that determines exactly how we will behave, who we will mix with, what we will try and what we will avoid. Every thought and every action stems from the way we see ourselves.

If I have a bad self-image, I will put up with all kinds of garbage and abuse from just about everybody. In the back of my mind will be thoughts like, "I don't matter that much, it's only me, and I have always been treated badly. Perhaps I deserve it."

Poppy Wants a Partner

Poppy is attractive, intelligent and desperately wants to get married. She meets Andy in a bar and they begin to date. Everything is wonderful for six weeks and then for no known reason, they have a massive argument. Exit Andy.

She discovers Barry. They date joyously for a month and a half – and then suddenly Barry decides to reunite with his ex-girlfriend. Exit Barry.

Poppy meets Cosmo online. Everything is blissful and romantic for a month or two and there is even talk of marriage. Then without warning, Cosmo disappears to

Mexico! And so Poppy's story continues through Dario, Emilio, Franco, Gino, Hugo, Ignacio, Jaroslav, Kieran, Levi, Mohammed...

All Poppy wants is a man to love her but it never quite happens.

Ted Wants a Trophy

Ted is a professional athlete. He has always seen himself as a quality competitor, but never as a national champion. Finally, after ten years of sweat and grind, Ted qualifies for the 400 metre final.

In the race of his life he explodes out of the blocks, pulls clear in the straight and leads the field into the final turn. Twenty metres from the line, with greatness within his grasp, he pulls a hamstring and hobbles home last.

Jim and Josie Want an Easy Life

Jim and Josie have been broke for as long as they can remember. Every day is a struggle to find rent money, pay kids' school fees and buy junk food. As they say, "Life wasn't meant to be easy." Then one day, their number comes up – they win a million dollars in the state lottery.

They buy an apartment *plus* furniture and an entertainment system. They get new cars. They take an around-the-world cruise and invest the remaining $300,000 with a good friend who is an "investment expert."

The good friend disappears to Mexico with the $300,000! (It's Cosmo!) Soon they are borrowing from the bank just to make their car payments. Short of cash, they sell the apartment during a slump and pawn the big screen TV. Inside two years they are broke. Jim says, "Life just doesn't seem fair!"

Why Do We Repeat Patterns?

Why does such "misfortune" happen to good people – including us? Here's why – and this is at the root of everything...

What you achieve and what you receive are entirely dependent on your thinking. All of your thoughts are shaped by your self-image. If at the deepest level you believe you don't deserve something, then you will either a) never get it or b) get it and lose it.

For Poppy to have a beautiful long-term relationship she has to believe that she is lovable *and* that it is possible. We are not talking "lip-service *I deserve it,*" we are talking "in-the-very-core-of-her being *I deserve it.*"

For Ted to take home the trophy, he has to see himself as a champion. He has to *feel* that he is the best. Any thoughts that "I'm really not good enough" or "this could never happen to me" will consistently sabotage a lifetime of training.

Jim and Josie will tell you they want an easy life. But if they believe that life should be difficult, if they believe that God will love them if they struggle, then they will find a way to struggle – whether they win one million dollars or 100 million.

Bank robbers are the perfect example of the self-image sabotaging prosperity. Most bank robbers don't look in the mirror each morning and say, "Life is beautiful. I love and accept myself." Most armed robbers grow up in homes that are low on cash and high on abuse. When you believe, "Life is unfair and I'm always broke," you find creative ways to squander suitcases full of cash in a weekend. It's not a *financial management problem*, it is *a self-image problem*.

You might say, "Their self-image is not the issue. The trouble is that they hang out with nasty people who like to shoot each other." But it is their self-image that determines the company they keep.

Boxers often come from backgrounds of poverty and violence. Stories of world champions who made millions and died broke are commonplace. Mike Tyson made and lost about US$300 million. It wasn't one bad investment decision.

Annie's Story
Even the cutest guy looks pretty ugly when he's banging your head against the wall.

For nearly 20 years I was beaten and abused by men. I am still piecing together how this happened and why I let it continue.

I was raised in a small country town, one of four children in a devout Christian family. I was an adventurous child and this often got me into trouble. To compensate, I would do things for my parents to try to make them proud of me. For example, our strict faith prohibited us from celebrating birthdays or Christmas, but there were no rules about wedding anniversaries. I loved to make my parents breakfast on their anniversary – but even then I would sometimes create more trouble – like the time that I forgot to put water in the electric kettle and blew it up. No matter how hard I tried, I never seemed to get it right.

I began high school as an outgoing and confident young teenager and my ambition was to become a teacher. Curious and somewhat rebellious, my quest for popularity sometimes led me into bad company.

Then at 14 I was raped.

Confused and ashamed, I told nobody. But my parents, my school and my church soon found out and it was a great source of shame to my parents and the church. I was called before the church elders to apologise. I couldn't understand why I should apologise. That would be admitting that it was *my fault* and it wasn't my fault.

I refused to apologise and I was *disfellowshipped* from the church.

Living at home with my parents became awkward, and as soon as I turned 16 I moved out to live with a girlfriend. Once the "A" student, I was now an outcast. I dropped out of school and went to work in an Asian grocery store. I worked two jobs but had little money, no skills and no family I could talk to. Within a year or so, my boyfriend, John, invited me to move to Melbourne with him. Melbourne sounded wonderful!

Into a Black Hole

John told me we would be staying in a house with one of his ex-girlfriends and her sister. It turned out that John was sleeping with *both* sisters – and I was girlfriend number three. I was given a mattress on the living room floor. John had sex with me during the day. At night he slept with the two sisters. I was a virtual prisoner in a violent house a thousand miles from home – so there I stayed for the next two years. I knew no one, I had no money and nowhere to go. I lived in fear of John's threats and beatings and with constant verbal abuse. Each day I feared for my life. I felt useless, worthless and unloved. I was heartbroken, humiliated and so, so sad.

"I would cut my arms just to feel the pain..."

It was like living in a black hole. When things are so lonely and bleak, you get numb. I began to cut myself. I had a pair of nail scissors and I would cut my arms just to feel the pain and watch the blood oozing down my wrists. It may seem strange, but at that time, it was the only way I knew to remind myself that I was alive – and that I could still feel. It seemed to me that I was slowly going insane.

I learned that John was a drug dealer connected with the triads and the Mafia. Heroin and cocaine were weighed and packaged on the kitchen table. John and I moved house several times – but although the address changed, the toxic mix of drugs and addicts, criminals and physical abuse remained constant.

It was while we were staying with an armed robber that I first tried to escape. I woke up one morning and decided, "I can't take this anymore!" I packed my bags and called a taxi. The cab arrived and pulled into the driveway, but just as I stepped into the cab, John arrived home and parked behind us. Trapped!

To teach me a lesson, he handcuffed me to a bed and left me for 48 hours in an empty house. Some months later I did escape.

More Abusive Relationships

A string of abusive relationships followed. At 24 I was engaged to be married. Two weeks before the wedding, my fiancé lost his temper and broke my nose. I might have gone through with the wedding but for a dear girlfriend who persuaded me that you don't marry people who break your nose.

Why have I been attracted to "bad" men and why did I stay with them? I don't fully understand myself. Certainly my poor self-image allowed me to put up with it. I had the idea that it was my fault – that if I just changed my behaviour, my boyfriends would love me.

Am I angry? I'm not angry any more. You can't change history. I have made some bad choices but they are behind me.

What Have I Learned?

- I have no reason to feel ashamed that I was raped.
- Acceptance is a powerful state of mind. To accept that something happened doesn't mean you agree with it.
- Following my rape I became quite promiscuous. I never wanted the sex, but I did want the hugs, I did want someone to think that I was nice and that I was pretty.
- I read in a book that some rape victims become anti-men and anti-sex, but that other women lose their self-respect and go the other way. This information explained a lot about my own behaviour and came as a great relief to me, because I thought there was something wrong with me.
- I used to think that if I showed affection to a guy, then I had to go all the way – otherwise I was guilty of leading him on. Now I know that what I want also matters. I can say "No" and he will get over it.
- Now that I like myself better, there is no hurry to get into relationships. I used to look for the

best-looking guy at a party, start a relationship with him – and then find out all about him! I discovered that even the cutest guy looks pretty ugly when he's banging your head against the wall.

- I now have a list on my refrigerator of all the things I value in a partner: loyalty, honesty, communication, trust. Good looks didn't even make the list.
- If a guy lies to you early in the relationship – if he tells you that he is single when he's married – then he will lie to you at the end of a relationship when he's having an affair with your best friend.

For reasons I can't explain I have always had a sense of purpose, and the feeling that I was meant to survive. Three years ago I made the decision to start a new life and live on my own. I began a new career in real estate and I have won several awards for my sales achievements. I now own my own home, my own four-wheel-drive and I have decided to spend a year travelling. I feel very proud.

I have left the past behind. Today I am a happy, free spirit and I like myself. I came a long way in three years.

Annie's email: Annie-happinessinhardtimes@live. com.au

Character

Did you ever look in the mirror and say, "I wish I had a different face… body… nose"? Did you ever ask yourself, "How come other people are so talented and brilliant?

How can I feel good about me?"

Most of us have these thoughts! Talent and beauty are useful – BUT there are plenty of talented and beautiful people around whom we don't necessarily admire. And some of them are a pain in the neck!

The qualities most of us value above all others are HONESTY, COURAGE, PERSISTENCE, GENEROSITY and HUMILITY.

Take a look at this list and you'll find something interesting. You aren't BORN with these things. You DEVELOP them. Anyone can have them. If you really want, you can have them! If you want self-respect, and respect from others, you don't have to be a genius or a super-model. You simply work at developing your own honesty, determination, generosity, humility and courage. It is called "character."

In a Nutshell
How you feel about you is in your hands.

Labels

Much of our stress comes from the labels we put on ourselves.

We tell ourselves, "I'm a wife" – so when we get divorced, we feel like failures. We tell ourselves, "I'm an executive" – so when we get the sack, we feel like failures. We tell ourselves, "I'm an achiever" – so when we fail, we feel like failures!

If my story is, "I'm the perfect host," I set myself up for misery because no evening is perfect. When the neighbours come to dinner and I burn the carrots, I'm devastated.

You are not your story and nobody cares anyway. You don't belong in a category or a box. You are a human being having a series of experiences. When you quit dragging a story around, you never have to look the part. You can relax.

Extraordinary achievers have an exceptional self-image. And here's the crunch: *the exceptional self-image comes first* – the life that unfolds is a result of the self-image. Nelson Mandela didn't change history and then decide, "I'm unique." Oprah Winfrey didn't build a media empire and then decide, "I'm special." People like these have a sense of entitlement. They expect life to bless them, they expect extraordinary experiences. They don't put up with crap.

Fred says, "If I could just get out of this hellhole, if I could just become an executive, if I could just marry a model, then I would have a good self-image." No Fred, you have to fix your self-image first. Happy and successful people know what they want and they feel they deserve it – it's called healthy self-appreciation.

It doesn't matter how much you know. It doesn't matter how many books you have read or how many positive quotes you have pinned on your wall. If you don't appreciate yourself you will not allow the things you want into your life. You have to feel you deserve it.

In a nutshell
You attract that which you are.

You Can Do It!

You say, how could I ever love myself enough to get what I want? Well, as a matter of fact, you can and you did. When you were two months old you loved yourself. But you let parents, teachers and preachers change your mind.

As a baby you were a powerful creature. You had no skills or education but you knew exactly what you wanted and you felt entitled to get it. As a result, you got it.

At two months you didn't talk – but if you could have, do you think you would have said to your parents, "Look, I know that I'm a pain and I cause you a lot of inconvenience. And I may not be deserving and I feel terrible for asking – but if it's not too much trouble, can someone get me a drink?" You wouldn't have! So why do it now?

Babies have a healthy self-appreciation. As a result babies get what they want when they want it. If you want to live a charmed life you need to think more like you did when you were two feet tall. You deserved love and nurturing when you were born and you deserve it now. Too many people get the idea that unless they are as clever or as smart or as handsome or as highly paid or as sporty or as witty as other people they know, they are undeserving of love and respect.

Too rarely do we focus on our real inner beauty. We let others convince us that we are unworthy. We buy into the idea that we are sinners. We become self-critical, believing that self-criticism is humility. SELF-CRITICISM

ISN'T HUMILITY – IT IS STUPIDITY.

Do you recall watching boy meets girl movies? As the boy and girl struggled through thick and thin, you hoped and prayed that everything would work out. He went to war, she left home, he came back, she was gone, he found her, her father told him to get lost, she told him to get lost, and all the time you hoped that they would live happily ever after. They got married and strolled off into the sunset as the curtain came down. You dried your tears and clutching your empty popcorn bucket, strolled out of the theatre.

We cry at those movies because at our deepest level, we care. We love. We are touched. There is that core in each of us that is simply beautiful. Depending on how much we have been hurt, we will conceal or reveal our deepest feelings, but we all have these qualities.

When we see the news stories about the starving around the globe, we all ache inside. We all care. That is the way we are. Accept that you have these qualities – the capacity to love and empathise and be human. You are not "only human". You *are human*. Recognise your own worth and remind yourself that you deserve to be treated well.

Most of us have a list – we say, "I would love myself if I wasn't ugly, I would love myself if I was more successful, I would love myself if I didn't binge, I would love myself if I didn't get angry, I would love myself if I could live up to God's standards."

We crave compliments but as quickly as we receive them, we dismiss them. Twenty-seven people tell you that you are wonderful and you are thirsty for it like a vampire. Then one person tells you bad stuff – who do you believe?

If I work hard, people will love me.

I grew up believing that *if you work hard, you are a good person.* So my whole life I found excuses to work longer and harder. Other authors write books. I found a way to work twice as hard – I write *and* illustrate books.

Other people leave their work at the office. I take mine on vacation – I find myself writing speeches by the pool. Of course I always have a brilliant excuse, "I just need to finish this and then I can relax." Some people do other people's work because they think *only they* can do it. I do other people's work even when they can do it better than me!

Julie will say to me, "You are *paying the taxi driver* – why are you loading our bags into the cab?" And I will have an excuse, "We are late for the airport," "This driver is too old," or "I need the exercise." But the truth is that my self-image is lacking. I'm not good at being spoiled. I believe I have to work hard for people to like me and for me to like me. But I am making progress.

Excuses or Results

We always have excuses: reasons why we are broke, reasons why we are lonely, reasons why we are working 70 hours a week. We pretend, "I'm not the problem. The world is doing this to me." If history keeps repeating itself, it's you that's making your history! If you have

been broke, lonely or exhausted for half your life, or for five years, or even six months, it's *you that's causing it* and it's *your self-image that's driving it.*

The good news is that when we a) take responsibility for a pattern, and b) change how we think about ourselves, we see instant improvement in how life and people treat us.

Any of the following indicate that we have work to do on our self image:

Self-Criticism
Self-talk like, "I am not smart enough... I should work harder... I am not worthy... I'm boring, ugly, stupid."

Criticising Others
When we are critical of others it really means that we don't like ourselves.

Comparing Ourselves with Others
When we constantly compare ourselves with others,

it is a sign that we don't accept ourselves. When we compare, we will always find someone who is better at something. Whenever we compare, we lose. Did you ever compare yourself and come out exactly equal?

Putting Others' Opinions Ahead of Our Own

What you think of you is more important than what anyone else thinks of you! Many people don't even believe they have the right to choose what is best for them. But if you don't have the right to choose what is right for you, who has?

Explaining and Justifying Ourselves

Whenever we justify our behaviour, it is really ourselves that we are trying to convince. You don't need to explain and justify yourself to anybody.

Going Without

When we fail to ask for what we want, when we discount our own needs or starve ourselves of luxuries unnecessarily, it's a sign of poor self-image.

Other indications that our self-image needs work:

- jealousy
- guilt
- failure to give or accept compliments
- inability to show or enjoy affection
- constant poor health
- insisting that we are always right.

While we concentrate on our own faults, the world will keep punishing us, and we will keep punishing ourselves. We do it with ill health, with poverty, with loneliness. As long as we don't like ourselves, the world won't like us. And then we blame the world.

In a Nutshell

It is no one else's responsibility to love you. It is your responsibility to love yourself.

So How Do I Turn This Around?

How do you feel when you nurse a baby or play with a puppy? Suddenly you are entranced, you see beauty – and as you appreciate the baby or the puppy, you are uplifted. Immediately you feel better about yourself. The principle is: noticing good things outside of yourself makes you feel better inside.

When you look for good things in other people, you find those things in yourself. THE FAST TRACK TO SELF-APPRECIATION IS IN APPRECIATING OTHERS.

As you look for beauty all around you, you feel happier with yourself. As you give compliments to others, you feel happier with yourself. We grow up believing that if you compliment people, you lose. They feel *better* and you feel *worse!* But when you compliment people, everybody wins. It's like magic. As you look for good things in everyone you meet, your life will change accordingly.

Tony Bennett is a role model for all of us. Tony is one of the most enduring, best loved, most admired and happiest people in show business. When Tony Bennett is on stage he acknowledges every member of his band, he praises the songwriters who created his music, he shares his love for the songs that propelled his career and of course, he thanks the audience. It is not flattery. It is deep, genuine appreciation. Listen to an interview with

Tony – he is an appreciation machine.

Appreciate others and they will appreciate you. It is no surprise that Tony Bennett has been so successful for so long.

Affirmations

How would you feel about looking into the bathroom mirror each morning and saying, "I love myself. I am confident and successful"?

Positive affirmations are one of the surest ways to program your subconscious for the life you want and deserve.

Let's say that you are feeling lonely and sad. So you give yourself an exercise: two minutes every morning for one month you look yourself in the mirror and repeat the following, "I love myself. I have wonderful friends who love and nurture me. I am always in the right place at the right time. I deserve to be happy."

Now, for the first few days you will probably feel silly. After a week you will feel more comfortable and after a month it may feel perfectly normal. Most importantly, you will see changes in your life.

Now I know you are wondering, "Can I really do this and what happens if my Mum sees me?" Don't worry about your Mum. This stuff works. Your subconscious mind accepts whatever you tell it. How you feel about yourself becomes your reality.

If you *feel lonely*, all you can attract is more loneliness.

If you *feel broke*, all you can attract is more poverty. Somehow you have to break the vicious cycle and you can do this with affirmations. As your feelings change, what you attract changes.

You can also *write* affirmations. Get up 20 minutes earlier and write pages and pages about how you want to be, for example:

- I am confident and happy
- I am a wonderful wife and a caring mother
- I have £50,000 in the bank
- I love my job.

Here's one simple affirmation that you can use for the rest of your life, "I love myself." Commit to it. When you feel depressed, when you feel despondent, "I love myself." When you are trying to love someone and you can't, love yourself instead. When you are feeling guilty, stupid, imperfect, tell yourself, "I love myself. I am imperfect and that is perfect!"

Also:

Always Speak Well of Yourself

If you have nothing good to say about yourself keep your mouth shut.

Accept Compliments

Always say "Thank you" or words to that effect.

Separate Your Behaviour from Yourself

Stop seeing yourself as guilty. Your behaviour is not connected to your self-worth. If you do something stupid, it doesn't make you a bad person. You simply made a mistake. Loving yourself means forgiving yourself. It means admitting that to this point you've lived your life the best way you know how.

And how do you know you are making progress? When you can say "I love myself while I'm feeling jealous," "I love myself even as I'm getting angry," "I love myself whilst I'm feeling hopeless." FORGET PERFECTION and AIM FOR IMPROVEMENT.

Be Assertive When Necessary
When other people are disrespectful, let them know how you expect to be treated.

Practise Having Pleasure Without Guilt
When your life is working out, tell yourself, "I deserve this!" The airline upgrades you to first class, you get a pay rise, a friend cooks you dinner – tell yourself, "I deserve it and there is more coming."

Nurture Yourself
Do things, wear things, eat things that make you feel good. Spend time with uplifting people. Also, if you have ever had someone in your life who adored you – your mother, the babysitter, an ex-girlfriend – make a habit of recalling the loving things they said to you.

In a Nutshell
People treat you as you treat you, the world treats you as you treat you.

5

Relationships

"If my husband would just love me a bit more, then I could like myself! Then maybe I might even love myself!"

If you are waiting for somebody to appreciate you before you appreciate yourself, then it is never going to happen.

Some people are uncomfortable with the idea of *loving themselves*. At the same time, they expect their partners to love them! Isn't that a little odd? To say, *"I couldn't possibly love myself,"* and then get angry with my wife when she doesn't love me? If you want someone to love you, you have to at least *like yourself!*

When we are preoccupied by our own faults, we look for the *same faults* in other people in the hope it will make us feel better. And we find them, but we don't feel better.

When we forgive ourselves for our own shortcomings, we automatically begin to let others off the hook for the same things.

PEOPLE REFLECT BACK TO US WHAT WE ARE. *The issue is always with ourselves.*

For the sake of our children, we have to accept ourselves. Children follow our example. If you give yourself a hard time, they'll give themselves a hard time – and they'll give you a hard time too!

In a Nutshell
When we forgive ourselves, we stop criticising other people.

If only I could have some quality people in my life...

We might look at our lives and say, *"If I didn't have to deal with my lazy husband and these rowdy kids, I could get on with my personal growth..."* Wrong! They are your personal growth.

The people in our lives are our teachers. Husbands who snore and leave cupboard doors open, "ungrateful" children, neighbours who park across the driveway... Only for so long can we tell ourselves, "I'd be happier if these guys got their act together!"

If your wife makes you angry, then your project is to deal with anger effectively. And you have the perfect person to help you do it right in your home. A practice partner! What fortune!

You might say, "I'll divorce her! That will fix it!" But it

will fix it only until you marry someone else who makes you just as angry.

> **In a Nutshell**
> Every person who walks into your life is a teacher. Even if they drive you nuts, they teach you because they show you where your limits are. Just because people are your teachers doesn't mean you have to like them.

It's Not the Job...

You'll notice something about good nurses – they like people even more than medicine. There is a clue here about finding meaning in your career. THE JOB ISN'T IT! Whatever you do for a living is a vehicle to connect with people. Whether or not you are fulfilled depends on how you serve the *people*. Albert Schweitzer said, *"... the only ones among you who will be truly happy will be those who have sought and found how to serve."*

"Serving people" sounds like slavery or sacrifice. It's not. It is simply knowing that there's joy in giving something of yourself which is uniquely yours. "Serving" can be teaching or nursing people. It can be selling them beautiful flowers or repairing their radiators with a smile. It's not about your job description. It's about your philosophy.

Society often evaluates careers in terms of PhDs and masters degrees, and we are in danger of missing the point. It's the people connections.

Let's say you are coaching a basketball team of 12-year-olds. You might love basketball and that's fine. But as soon as you understand that *it's not about basketball at all*, then you can really do something for those kids. You might say, "Basketball coaches don't change the lives of 12-year-olds." Wrong! Some do – and they are the coaches who understand they are teaching kids about life, and basketball is just the excuse.

Meanwhile, too many teachers tell themselves, "What do I matter? The kids don't care about algebra." Of course they don't! If you are teaching sixth grade, your mission is not algebra. It is children. If you are a banker, your mission isn't balance sheets, it's people.

Cherry's Story

To me the sound of a metal cap being unscrewed from a glass bottle is the worst sound in the world. To my husband it is heaven.

Between these two sentences lies my story.

Kevin was a big, cuddly man with very dark eyes that left you wondering where his pupils were. A quiet, gentle person, he spoke softly and sparingly. There was a touch of mystery about him. When he walked into a room no-one else mattered. I loved him dearly. We were married in 1970 and Kim our only daughter was born in 1973.

Kevin was kind and caring; when I was ill he would cook and hang out the washing; when our daughter Kim was born, he was the one to feed her at night. He would give me surprises and thoughtful presents. He was a respectful and honest man who had no time for trivia, "give me the bottom line" was a favourite phrase. He held a top government job, and at work he was liked and respected.

I loved his dry humour. When our favourite cat died and we were all so upset, Kevin remarked, "When I'm gone I hope you will miss me as much as that cat."

Drink Becomes a Problem

Kevin always drank a little more than most but rarely to excess. But after his mother's death and a restructure at his workplace, I noticed him drinking more. Whenever I voiced my concerns Kevin would say, "You're exaggerating."

Social occasions became embarrassing and he would get aggressive if any comment was made about his drinking. By 2000 Kevin was constantly unwell, and he drank more and more. Some weekends, he would withdraw all the money from the ATM and go on a binge. Come Monday morning, I would be at the bank to get the account out of overdraft. This became a familiar pattern.

> "Somehow a good man had disappeared before my eyes."

He would go for groceries and come home drunk, without groceries. He would go to the office and come home drunk. If I didn't hand over our ATM card, he would threaten me. I was constantly ashamed, embarrassed, often angry, but also very saddened that Kevin had come to this. Somehow a good man had disappeared before my eyes.

In 2000 Kevin booked in for a hospital detox program. He emerged ten days later as a man seeing the world for the first time. He apologised for letting us down so badly. He promised to be different. He told us, "I'm so lucky to have a family to come back to, to have a house and a job still waiting."

Things were better for a while. June 2001 saw Kevin diagnosed with Hodgkin's disease and he began treatment. Despite the odds and his damaged body, his health improved. Kevin swore he had learnt his lesson. But as his health returned so did the drinking. He promised to quit. I lived in hope. I felt like I was married to a stranger. He still looked the same, sometimes sounded the same, but he had become someone else. He was unreliable. He had become a liar and a bully. He enrolled in more detox programs in 2003, 2004, 2006. I tried leaving him, I tried going back. As the drink tightened its grip he became more abusive. He was so big and I am a small woman and I feared for my safety.

I had endless conflicting conversations in my head and I began to wonder if I was going mad, "Am I exaggerating the problem? No, I'm not. It really is that bad! But I know how nice he can be. If I keep quiet, if I keep trying to find help for him, it will turn around –"

Whatever happened to the man I loved?
Sometimes we are surrounded by the evidence but we

deny the inevitable – until something finally happens and we realise, "There is no hope."

The penny dropped for me when Sam, our youngest granddaughter came to spend a day with us. Kevin idolised Sam. They spent the morning in the garden potting out vegetable plants, and when they came in for lunch I noticed he had been drinking. With the excuse that he was going for cigarettes, Kevin left the house and returned more drunk. That night I found two vodka bottles in the car – one under the driver's seat and one stashed in the spare wheel. In that moment I understood, "If he won't stop drinking for one day for the granddaughter that he loves and adores, he's not going to stop for anyone."

I once heard alcoholics described as psychological vampires. It is true. They drain your vitality, your happiness and your bank balance. The constant stress of the unknown, day after day, sucks the life out of you. The books told me, "Your husband is sick." All I knew was that he was making me sick too!

Even if you love someone with all your heart you shouldn't have to suffer their abuse. You don't deserve abuse from your friends or from your family – and you don't deserve it from your partner. One final weekend in January 2005, Kevin was lurching around the house in an angry, drunken stupor. He screamed at me, "*Get out. I want to do what I want, when I want. Get out!*"

I packed my things into cardboard boxes, threw all my clothes on the back seat of my car and drove away. I never went back.

There's something surreal about leaving the home that you have known for 30 years. I felt numb – like my foundations had collapsed from under me. I never dreamt this would happen. But ultimately there was a huge sense of relief. I no longer dreaded going to sleep at night and I no longer feared for my safety. A heavy weight had been lifted from my shoulders and I could breathe freely. Slowly the sun came out.

Helping People

It is natural to want to help people, to care for someone who is ill, to do what is expected of us – but for how long? And what if the other person doesn't want our help?

At first I thought Kevin needed me to stay with him, that maybe he would die if I didn't stay, and that it would be my fault. But we cannot be responsible for another human being choosing to live or die. If Kevin did die from drinking two bottles of vodka in a day, that would be his choice, his responsibility and his life.

> *"Everything I tried to do to help or change my husband did nothing"*

Everything I tried to do to help or change my husband did nothing. Leaving was traumatic and scary. But staying was worse.

Things went downhill quickly for Kevin. He was convicted of drink driving, he lost his job, he fell down the stairs and hurt his head, there were visits to hospital, our home was sold up. He became depressed, defeated and hollow. His dignity was gone. It was so sad to watch him self-destruct.

By 2007 Kevin's medical problems were extreme. He had intense pain in his legs, he couldn't walk, couldn't sleep except in short bursts and his short-term memory was shot. He died peacefully in his sleep on 28 October 2007. It saddened me greatly that he chose alcohol over his family that loved and respected him – and still does.

What Other People Think

For some unknown reason we believe we must present a perfect image to the world – to the great "they" out there. We think that people are watching and judging us. Looking back, I really don't know who "they" are, and if I could have named those people, did they really care?

Everyone is not talking about you; they have enough problems of their own. They may stop for a few moments and say, "Goodness, who would have thought that!" And then they drift back to issues that matter to them more, like "What's for dinner?" Your problems are not important to other people.

I still love and miss the man that Kevin was – but not the man he became. I now live in a separate self-contained unit attached to the home of my daughter and son-in-law and their two daughters. I will be eternally grateful to Kim and her husband. Where once I was sad and desperate, I now enjoy a stress-free, loving environment full of laughter and optimism. I work part time and I have written a series of books on patchwork. I recently published my new book about life with Kevin – *My Concrete Umbrella* – in the hope that

I can help others who live with an alcoholic partner. I came through hard times.

Cherry's website: www.myconcreteumbrella.com

Who are we to judge?

Often we figure we know what is best for other people – but they take a different road altogether.

If people don't ask your advice, they don't want it. If people ask your advice and then ignore it, they don't want it.

When People Get Divorced

Karen and Ken dated for three years and were married for ten. They travelled the world, they have two beautiful children, they enjoyed dinners with their friends and family. They had a lot of fun.

After 11 good years together, they separated. Now all she can say is, "He was a lousy lover and he has a small dick!"

What about all the good times? If you fell in love with somebody, if you married them, lived with them, shared a life with them, then you had good times. Speak well of them. Remember the good times!

Blaming and Forgiveness

"All blame is a waste of time. You may succeed in making another feel guilty but you won't succeed in changing whatever is making you unhappy." Dr Wayne Dyer

At some point most of us learned that it is a good idea to forgive people. We learned that it is "holy" or "spiritual." But there is a more basic reason to forgive people: when you *don't* forgive them, it ruins your life!

Let's say:

a) you are my boss and you give me the sack, or

b) you are my girl, and you run off with my buddy.

So I say, "I'll never forgive you for that!"

Who suffers? Not you! I'm pacing the floor. I've got a knot in my stomach. I'm losing sleep. I'm carrying around the toxic poison in my system. You are probably out partying! Where do we get the idea that if WE don't forgive people, THEY suffer? It's nuts!

Studies at the Public Health Institute in California confirm that hostility and resentment tear down your immune system and double your risk of heart attack, cancer and even diabetes. Bitterness makes you sick!

To forgive someone, you don't have to agree with what they did. You just have to want your life to work.

Here's what happens. We create rules in our head for how people should behave. When people break the rules, we resent them. Resenting people for ignoring our rules is absurd. Next time you are resenting someone, close your eyes and experience your feelings. Experience your body. Making people guilty makes you miserable.

People do what they do, knowing what they know. Whether you make them guilty, makes no difference – except that *it ruins your life*. Things are the way they are. If a hurricane floods your basement, do you say, "I'll never forgive the weather?" If a seagull craps on your head, do you resent the seagull? Then why resent people? We are no more meant to control people than we are meant to control rainstorms and seagulls. The universe doesn't operate on guilt and blame – guilt and blame are just stuff we've made up.

While we're talking about forgiveness, the first step to making your life work is to forgive your parents. Sure they weren't perfect. But they had a lot of other things to worry about besides raising you! Whatever they got wrong, it is history.

Some people never forgive their parents and mess up their lives just to demonstrate to their parents what a lousy job they did. Their message is, "It's your fault that I am broke and lonely and unhappy so now you can watch me suffer!" Every day that you refuse to forgive your mother is a vote to screw up your life.

In a Nutshell
Forgiveness is a gift you give yourself.

What if someone does something terrible? Do I forgive him?

I told this story in *Follow Your Heart* and it is worth repeating. I have a friend called Sandy McGregor. In January 1987, a young man with a shotgun walked into Sandy's living room and murdered his three teenage daughters. The tragedy saw Sandy descend into a personal hell of pain and anger. Few of us could imagine what he went through.

With time, and the help of friends, he decided that his only chance to make his life work was to let go of the anger, and somehow forgive the offender. Sandy now spends his life helping others to achieve forgiveness and peace of mind. His experience is evidence that it is humanly possible to let go of our resentments, even in the most horrific circumstances. Sandy would also tell you that he let go of his anger for his own benefit and his own survival.

I notice that people who have had experiences like Sandy, fall into roughly two groups. The first group remain prisoners of their own anger and bitterness. The second group achieve an uncommon depth and compassion.

The events that transform us are usually not the things we would choose. As someone said, we never want to go through what we need to go through, to become what we want to become. Heartbreak, illness, loneliness, desperation... we each get our share. After any major loss, there is always a mourning process. But ultimately, the question is whether the experience makes you harder or softer.

For those of us who are less challenged than Sandy, the choice is the same. "Do you want your life to work or don't you?"

I'll Never Forgive Myself!

If forgiving others is difficult, forgiving ourselves is even harder. We can spend a lifetime punishing ourselves mentally and physically for what we believe to be our own shortcomings. We may over-eat or under-eat, drink ourselves into oblivion, systematically destroy all our relationships or live in poverty. At the root of this suffering can be a belief system that says, "I have done a lot of bad things," "I am guilty" or "I don't deserve to be healthy and happy."

If you are feeling guilty you have already put yourself through enough. Why prolong it? If you were to feel guilty for another year or two, would it help?

Giving

How often do people *give* and then get angry? Fred says, "I gave my kids a car but what do they do for me?" So was it a gift, Fred, or was it something else?

If you give and want something in return, it is not a gift, it is an *arrangement*. If there are strings attached, tell your kids, "I am buying you this car but this is what I want – I want one phone call per week, one meal a month – plus, at least once a year you need to tell me that you are grateful. Otherwise I will resent you."

You say, "Wait a minute, if I give somebody something, they *should* be grateful." Well, you can believe that but it won't help you to be happy!

I learn from my friend Frank. Frank is a generous guy. When his family are in trouble, he helps out. When his brother Carlo lost all his money at the casino and was deep in debt, Frank borrowed money and gave it to Carlo so he could pay his debts. I asked Frank, "How did you feel about borrowing $200,000 to give to your brother?" Frank said, "I'd rather be in *my* position borrowing it than in *his* position needing it."

In a Nutshell

The joy of giving is in the moment. Once you have given, it is over. If you want to be happy there is only one way to give – expect nothing back.

Gratitude to Parents

Being a child means that you have parents who help you out. From the day you are born they are there to feed you, clothe you, buy you toys, loan you cars, give you money. The whole arrangement can become a one-way street. Parents keep giving and giving and kids figure, "That's your job."

We might argue, *children should be grateful.* But in reality, most children have no idea what their parents have done for them, myself included. My parents both passed away 20 years ago and I've had 20 years to think about what they did for me. If they were here now I would tell them how grateful I am. I would do things differently. But I am like most of the world's children who *didn't have a clue* until *I didn't have my parents.*

Parents complain that they are unappreciated. They ARE unappreciated and that seems to be how the world works. Most children never repay their debt to their own parents. They give to the next generation.

When Money Makes People Unhappy

A neighbour came to see Julie. He said, "Would you publish my book about my father and what he did?"

She asked, "Was he a great man?"

"No, he was a rotten bastard. He died and gave me nothing. My brother got the farm."

(Julie never published the book.)

A similar story: Dick had a son and two daughters and they got along well enough. In his will, Dick gave *roughly* a third to each child, but he did give his *unmarried* daughter a bit more than the two married children. That's when the fight started! The kids haven't spoken to each other for six years. If Dick were still alive, the kids would still be talking. If Dick had left everything to the city museum, the kids would still be talking. But because the division wasn't quite even, the family disintegrated.

Happy families are torn apart by wills and inheritances. They spend years in court and go to their graves angry – which creates more problems.

Where do we get the idea that we have a right to other people's money – even that we have a right to our parents' money?

In a Nutshell
Do you want to be happy? Decide now, "Nobody owes me anything. Whatever anybody gives me is a bonus."

6

Money

"I've Lost Everything!"

A man phoned Doctor Robert Schuller, the famous preacher. He moaned, "It's over. I'm finished. All my money has gone. I've lost everything."

Doctor Schuller asked, "Can you still see?"

The man replied, "Yes, I can still see."

Schuller asked, "Can you still walk?"

The man said, "Yes, I can still walk."

Schuller said, "Obviously you can still hear or you wouldn't have phoned me."

"Yes, I can still hear."

"Well," Schuller said, "I figure you have got about everything left. All you have lost is your money."

You probably appreciate Dr Schullers' point – money isn't everything. You probably also empathise with the man who lost his cash!

People fall into two major groups – those who have money and say, "MONEY'S NOT THAT IMPORTANT," and those who don't have money and say, "MONEY'S VERY IMPORTANT." There is another group – those who PRETEND MONEY IS NOT IMPORTANT but never pay for coffee.

We see news stories of barefoot children in poor countries and we say, "They have nothing but they are happy!" They are happy but that is no argument for you to be poor! If you are a ten-year-old Somalian who has never owned a book or heard of laptops or decent health care, it is easier to be content. It is also easier to be content when you are the child – it is tougher for the parents.

Here's what studies in developing countries show about money and happiness: a family needs a certain amount to take care of essentials – bread, clothing, shelter – let's say the amount is £15,000 per year. People with much less than that report increasing happiness as their income climbs, up to about £15,000. After £15,000 their happiness increases only slightly as their income continues to rise.

In other words, once your basic needs are met, twice as much money won't make you twice as happy. This explains why Warren Buffet seems cheery enough – but probably not 62 billion times happier than you.

So is money important? It's not important if you want to live in a cave.

But if you want to join the 21st century, you need it. Money gives you choices. When your mother is sick, you can buy a plane ticket to visit her. You can buy decent shoes for your children. With money, you can get your brakes fixed. You can get your teeth fixed so your breath won't smell! Sometimes having money will save someone's life – maybe your own. That's useful.

Of course, there are emotional scars and health problems that money won't fix. That's no reason not to have it. When you have enough money, you can concentrate on other more important things. Oscar Wilde noted, "The only people who think more about money than the rich are the poor."

It's Good To Make Money

The best thing that you can do for the poor is to not be one of them!

Some people are uncomfortable with money. Really! So let's get one thing straight – it is okay to have plenty of money. Then you can actually help the poor. You can also help yourself.

**"Money itself won't make you happy.
The joy is in having more than other people."**

Most of us know what it's like to be broke. I do. I know what it's like to be driving your old car and you hear a new noise. It sounds something like a tumble drier, and you get that sick feeling. You say to yourself, "If this costs more than $50 to fix, I'll be walking."

It's better to have money than not have it. If you are going to take the trouble of going to a restaurant, you might as well eat what you really want, rather than have to eat the cheapest thing on the menu. It's better to travel in comfort than to travel in the luggage rack.

How many of us grow up believing, "If I have plenty, others will go without." This is the silliest belief of all, "If I'm prosperous, other people will suffer." You know who spreads that idea? The people who don't have it! It's nuts.

If Santa Claus came down your chimney and dropped a million pounds cash on your coffee table, would it stay there? I don't think so! Your local restaurants would get some of it, the local car dealer might see some, together with your local cinemas, supermarkets, travel agents, the tax man and the telemarketers from Bangalore. People all around you would benefit.

Yet many of us grow up believing it's not okay to be prosperous because it will deprive other people. If you get prosperous, it doesn't have to hurt other people. It can help them.

In a Nutshell
Most people are more embarrassed by money than sex.

We like nothing more than a miserable millionaire

For you to be rich, you need to be happy that other people are rich. If you don't like rich people, or if you think all rich people are dirty bastards, then you will never allow yourself to be rich because subconsciously, you don't want to be a dirty bastard.

Imagine you met someone at a party who told you quite matter-of-factly: "My wife and I just flew in from Paris in our Lear jet – we were buying diamonds." Would your first thought be, "This guy is loaded. How wonderful for him!" Or would it be, "I bet he sells drugs, the dirty bastard."

Gossip magazines thrive on stories about rich people who aren't happy... "Jen made 20 million last year but she can't keep a man"... "Frank is fifth on the Forbes Rich List but he's dying of prosperitosis!"

If every rich person you ever met was a miserable sod, you might conclude that prosperity and happiness don't go together. This might be a subconscious conclusion but it will keep you poor. If you "know" that money and happiness don't mix, then you will work hard to stay poor.

The truth is, some very wealthy people enjoy loving relationships and are very happy. For you to be prosperous and happy, you need be happy that they are happy.

Choosing to be Broke!

Now this is interesting... some people would rather stay broke! Really! You say, "Why would anyone want to be broke?" Some people want to... and they have their reasons.

For example:

If I grew up believing, "GOD WILL LOVE ME IF I AM POOR." How would I feel about being rich? Scared stiff!

Because I wouldn't want God to think I'm greedy. The idea that "God will love me if I'm broke" keeps a lot of people broke.

What about if ALL MY FRIENDS ARE POOR? Would I want to be rich? Maybe not! Friends can get very angry when you start to be different. Rich is different. Friends can get very upset when you start to do well! I might decide better to be poor and keep my friends.

Or what if I GET SYMPATHY FROM PEOPLE FOR BEING POOR? What if sympathy is the only attention I get? What would happen if I suddenly became prosperous? Being poor might be safer.

Or what if I JUST DON'T WANT TO CHANGE MYSELF, change my thinking habits, my saving habits, my work habits? I might decide "poor is easier."

Or what if MONEY ONLY CAUSES ARGUMENTS? Example: Anne's childhood memories are of her parents arguing about money. So she decided early in life that money causes pain – and the only way to be happy was to avoid it. She chose a career where she would never need to discuss money or sell stuff. She has never invested a dollar and would sooner walk across hot coals than negotiate on the price of a car or a handbag.

Our Beliefs Keep Us Trapped

Take Fred. There is a bit of Fred in most of us. Fred's family was always short of money. His Dad told him, "Life is tough. Rich people are crooks!" So Fred will tell you what? "Life is tough."

In a Nutshell

Crazy as it sounds, some people choose poverty. They don't do it consciously, but when they make critical decisions that affect their prosperity, they end up doing what keeps them poor – and they don't even know it's happening. If you want to be prosperous, you need to flush out these subconscious ideas! They will keep you broke.

Now, Fred knows a few people who have money, but they make him feel uneasy. Fred's friends have no money, and they mostly blame their boss, the economy or the government. Fred likes to sit around with his friends and talk about how hard life is. He feels comfortable hanging out with people who agree that life is unfair!

Because Fred believes that life is a struggle, he only applies for lousy jobs with bad pay – because for Fred, that's normal. One day when Fred is looking through the employment section in the newspaper, he sees a position advertised in an office across the street... "flexible hours, exciting travel opportunities, company car, generous salary."

So what does Fred think? "No job is this good – there must be a catch!" He keeps looking.

He spots another advertisement, and this time the job is an hour's drive across town. No car, long hours, low pay. Fred says, "This is worth a closer look!" He attends an interview. The boss says, "Our products are revolting, our customers hate us, and the owner is a crook. If you want to work here you're nuts!"

And Fred says, "When can I start?"

"Just so you know – money doesn't make you happy!"

Fred stays there for 20 years. Fred knows that life is hard – and he can prove it to you! Fred also has a program in his head that says, "Fred, you never have any money." So every time he gets some spare cash, he spends it. Whenever he has a fistful of notes, his subconscious mind says, "This feels weird; having a full wallet! I had better buy something!" So he goes and buys a bigger TV, he takes a vacation and soon he's back to normal – broke! Then he can relax.

Fred is a caricature of half the population. He expects to be short of cash – and that is what he gets. In fact, that is what he creates. He has his list of reasons that explain his struggle. Fred says:

- "I never have any money because I never got a good education." He forgets that lots of university professors and other people with fancy degrees are poor – and other guys who were thrown out of school at 14 are very wealthy.
- "I've got the wrong job to become wealthy." He forgets that many people get themselves a sideline, or a hobby in order to make extra money. Others change jobs.
- "I don't have enough time to get wealthy." He forgets that everyone gets 24 hours in a day.
- "I would like to be prosperous but I don't want to work myself into the ground." But millions of people work long hours and stay poor. Some people work reasonable hours and get rich.

Hard work is an ingredient, but it doesn't guarantee wealth! If you have your head down plucking chickens in a chicken factory, ten hours a day, plucking more chickens won't make you much better off. At some stage what you will need is a change of strategy.

Now, if you suggest to Fred that he might want to "unbelieve" ideas that he has accepted for 40 years he will probably get very upset. He might think, "I've struggled for 40 years. You want me to admit that my life could have been different – that I helped create this?"

But Fred is not an exception to the rule. He is the rule – to which you need to be the exception. Our beliefs are like our own roadmap. We look at our map and say, it is possible to go here... but it is impossible to go there. So we only ever visit the places that are on our map.

Other people have a different map so they go to different places. What do poor people say? "My map is the only map!"

If you want to go to new places, you need a new map.

In a Nutshell

We become very attached to what we believe. Often, we would rather be right than happy – or we would rather be right than rich!

Alfred's Story

Growing up in Innsbruck, my teachers warned me about failure. They told me that if I failed at absolutely everything, I would end up a street sweeper. My father was a street sweeper. So I was always ashamed of my father. I was ashamed because he was ashamed. He drank to hide his shame. He wasn't the angry alcoholic, more the quiet unachiever.

As a kid I was surrounded by failure – mostly my own. Each year at school, I got the worst possible marks without having to repeat a grade. That was probably my greatest achievement.

I lived in fear and shame. At 15 a teacher got me a job in a bank licking stamps. I was totally out of place amongst men in suits – when I saw people in the corridor, I hid behind the cupboard. The bank would send me on ten minute errands to the post office. The post office was almost next door but I would take five hours. I wasn't misbehaving – I was just too terrified of the bank people to come back to work.

After five months of waiting five hours for me to find my way back from the post office, they sacked me.

My closest friends either died early or went to jail. I remember when Peter Fleischmann was charged with robbing a petrol station. He happily admitted to the crime but wanted to argue with the judge about how he had entered the premises. He told the court, "I'm a classy criminal – there is no way that I would crawl through the window of a toilet." They sent him to jail anyway.

At 17 I got a job as an apprentice sign writer. I loved painting signs and I was good at it – next to being an artist, which was my crazy dream, it seemed like the perfect job. I was the top apprentice in Austria three years running. This could have been the beginning of a better life but instead it nearly killed me.

Going Hungry

I wanted desperately to be somebody – not just a labourer, I wanted to be a businessman. So I started my own sign-writing business. I had no customers but I did have my own recipe for success. It was sheer genius: if you have no work, employ more people! As business plummeted, I expanded. Soon I had four employees. It amazes me that I was so stupid.

I would sleep all morning, leaving my four men sitting at the workshop with nothing to do. For weeks I wouldn't have a penny to buy even a potato. I starved. I remember scouring my apartment, desperate for anything to eat. I would find half-eaten slices of bread in the back of a drawer, cut off the green bits and soak them in water to make them chewable. I ate mouldy crusts that I found under the carpet. I was sick with stress. Every morning I coughed up a strange green slime. That was my green period.

> *"I would find half-eaten slices of bread in the back of a drawer, cut off the green bits and soak them in water to make them chewable."*

Somehow my "business" lasted five years. I was terrified, traumatised, immobilised and ultimately hospitalised. My symptoms looked like a heart attack but in fact I had a total nervous breakdown. I spent two months in hospital and by the time I was released, I had been declared bankrupt.

Having done very little for five years, I did absolutely nothing for the next two. I felt useless, everything seemed hopeless and I was still broke. It seemed like a good time to leave the country. I discovered Australia was looking for sign writers and decided to migrate. Australia needed me!

I made two critical decisions when I left Europe. I decided I would never again:

- spend money I don't have, or
- pretend to be someone I'm not.

Sometimes you meet someone who changes your destiny. In Australia, at age 32, I met Peter Matthews – he became both my best friend and the father I never had. Peter was a successful landscape artist. For the first time I saw that it was possible to make a living doing what I had only dreamed about. Peter didn't teach me how to paint. But he taught me how to think like a professional artist. Peter showed faith in me and by his example, taught me how to be a better person. These days "mentor" is a cliché – but that's what Peter was: my mentor.

Within a year or so I was selling my own paintings. I began teaching art and I was fortunate to win several art competitions. I was on my way.

I bought a house for $3,500. You've heard of buying the worst house in the street. I bought the worst house in the entire country – but I was over the moon. It took me a year to make it fit to live in. For the first time in my life, I owned something.

For the last 30 years I have earned my living by painting. I look back now and can't believe I survived, let alone prospered!

Growing up in poverty, I had fantasies of being an artist and sailing ocean yachts. Despite going broke and almost dying, I did become an artist. And today, when I'm not painting, I sail my yacht. No matter how low you go, there is hope.

Alfred's website: www.alfredengel.com

Attachment to Money

"Never be afraid of having nothing."
Abel Damoussi, Entrepreneur

While wealthy people focus on wealth, and a financial plan, it doesn't pay to be too desperate. This is a tricky concept to explain – there is a delicate balance to be struck between "being focused" and "being desperate." When you are too desperate, you somehow push away the very thing that you are chasing – whether it's boyfriends, opportunities – or money.

The more emotional you are about things, the less control you have. Most people are very emotional about money – so they are out of control, and they don't get much of it. In a sense we need to be able to live without something in order to have it. Once we can let go, we are in a position of power.

Successful negotiators know that the only way to pull off a successful deal is to become emotionally unattached. Most people who make a lot of money, only start to make buckets of it when they stop working for it! In other words, they find something they love to do, their attention is on giving service rather than the money itself, and the wealth flows automatically. They have money because they let go of it.

We might look at someone who is financially successful and say, "The greedy pig. He is worth 10 million and he is still working!" The man is working because he loves the challenge more than the money. That is why he is rich! Detachment is a major reason why rich people get richer. They don't care so much – they're not desperate.

If you don't have money, you've got to be relaxed enough to know you're going to get it. When you do have it, you need to be comfortable enough with it to keep some of it – and know there's more coming. Also, there's a big difference between a poor person's attitude – wishing you had it – and a wealthy person's attitude – believing you'll get it.

Whether you are applying for a job, doing a deal or selling a scooter, detach yourself. Give 100% effort – and at the same time, tell yourself, "I can live without this."

I know a fellow who used to wholesale denim jeans. Before a big sales call, he would arrive half an hour early and he would sit in the car park and talk to himself. He would tell himself, "I don't have to sell these trousers today. I don't need this deal. I don't care if they buy or not." By the time he walked into the meeting, he was unattached. He wasn't arrogant but he had let go of the outcome. Whatever happened, happened. And his sales went through the roof.

While you are desperate, while you are sitting on the edge of your seat, praying and holding your breath, nothing falls your way. It is principle. You know this. I think it is life's way of telling us not to be so serious. Prosperous people know how to let go.

7

Wealth

To make money, and keep it, you must be comfortable with money!

Increasing your prosperity is likely to be a long-term project. The journey is more an inside one than an outside one:

1. GET COMFORTABLE WITH MONEY. Be at ease talking about it, asking for it, giving it. Get comfortable with spare cash. If you are nervous even talking about money, if money doesn't sit well with you, you are never going to have it. It's not so much a conscious thing, it's a subconscious thing. Things we're awkward about, we avoid.

Have you ever noticed how hard it is to give some people money. They go crazy! "No, it's okay, really. I don't need it." You know they are living on bread and water! They change personality! They get embarrassed. They get insulted! "I don't need your money. I'm fine."

Imagine that:

- A friend of yours who has plenty of money wanted to give you £1,000. How would you react?
- You are out shopping with a colleague when you realise that you have left your wallet at home. Would you be comfortable saying, "Can I borrow some cash or put my purchases on your credit card?" Or would you have a panic attack and tell yourself, "I don't really need to buy anything today."

- You just sold your motorbike to your neighbour who paid you £4,000 cash. On the way to the bank you meet a friend and stop for coffee. Your friend notices that your wallet is absolutely stuffed with notes. Would you be perfectly comfortable being seen with a lot of money or would you hurriedly explain why it is that your wallet is as thick as a brick?

Many people don't have money because they're not at ease with it. As a rule, the more stressed you are about money, the less you'll have.

2. COLLECT YOUR BILLS. When people owe you money, you need to be comfortable about asking for it back.

Some of us have trouble even talking about money! We lend a friend a week's wages and when we need it back, we don't know how to ask for it – "Ah, you know that... do you remember... well... this isn't really important, and I don't really need it... and it doesn't matter if... how can I put this... I was just wondering about the..." – instead of asking in a sensible manner, "Can you return my money?"

3. CONSTANTLY RE-AFFIRM THAT YOU DESERVE TO BE PROSPEROUS. When the bills come in, re-affirm, "I have everything I need."

Many people spend their lives worrying about bills and complaining that they have no money. They create a subconscious pattern that says, "I'm always broke." And then they wonder why they don't have any money. If you always tell yourself you're broke, know that you will always be broke.

4. CARRY MONEY. Some people never carry any cash! How can you feel prosperous if your wallet is empty? If you want to feel prosperous, you need to carry money. Practise carrying around an extra £20 in your wallet – or at least £10 – that you never spend. When you get down to the last £10, add more.

You might say, "But if it's there, I spend it!" That's exactly why you should do it – to learn financial control. If you seriously want to learn about prosperity, trusting yourself with £10 is a good start.

Fred says, "What if someone steals my wallet?" What's the point in carrying an empty wallet and feeling broke and inconvenienced every day of your life – out of fear someone might steal ten pounds? That's no life.

"Stephen's had enough to eat – haven't you Stephen?"

Rich People Invest, Poor People Consume

My brother, sister and I were blessed with loving, sensible parents who knew how to stretch a dollar. Mum mended our socks, Dad owned one good suit, we grew our own tomatoes and we ate liver and sheeps' brains.

My parents gave us very sensible, but not very cool Christmas presents. I remember a conversation at school where a buddy asked, "Hey guys, what did you get for Christmas?"

Rob said, "A new water ski!"

Mal said, "A rifle."

And I said, "Pyjamas!"

When I was nine, I was the only kid in my class who didn't have a bike. All I wanted was a bike – any bike.

Across the paddock from our house lived the James family. There were three boys in the family. They not only had bikes, they had new bikes – those dragster bikes with gears. This was wealth beyond my comprehension! Three new dragster bikes in one family. The James were like… royalty!

My mother often gave away things to the needy. I came home one day to find some extra space in my closet. Mum explained, "I've just given some of your clothes to a family that is struggling to buy food."

And I said, "Who's that?"

Mum said, "The James."

"The James need my pyjamas?" She might as well have said, "Donald Trump!" I was flabbergasted. I would lie awake at night wondering, "How can a family with the best bicycles in the universe not afford to buy bread?" Eventually I came to understand that a) you create the problem when you buy the best bikes in the universe, and b) lots of people live like that.

Just because you buy something doesn't mean you can afford it. That's why people who can't pay their rent have the biggest TV sets.

At ten, I never saw the whole picture, which was: my parents owned their home, they paid cash for their cars, they always had enough for life's essentials and they never argued about money. The small price I paid was in Christmas pyjamas and waiting a bit longer for a bike. I eventually got a bike for my tenth birthday.

Of course, if you had asked me at nine, "Would you rather have a new bicycle or eat sheeps' brains?" the choice was obvious. But now I understand the wisdom behind my parents' strategy.

When I was older and more interested, Dad explained to me, "You only borrow money to buy things that will increase in value or make you money." He also explained, "Investments like real estate and quality shares give you an income and are likely to increase in value. Consumer goods like TVs and bicycles give you no income and decrease in value."

Which leads us to the question, "How many things that you have bought in the last ten years have increased in value?" Your answer will give you an idea as to whether you are on the road to wealth.

In a Nutshell

Wealthy people invest. Poor people consume. Your path to financial independence is a two-step process:
a) make the money (that's the easier bit)
b) change your habits – saving, spending, and investing habits (the hard bit).
Wealth is often simpler than we admit.

It's Not My Fault

I watched the following conversation unfold on TV between a distraught woman and a financial advisor:

Woman: My husband just lost his job and we don't know what we are going to do. We have a huge mortgage plus loans for two expensive cars. All these overpaid executives on Wall Street have created this global financial mess. It's not fair. The government should do something!

Expert: Your husband had a well-paid job?

Woman: Yes he did.

Expert: He got pay rises over the last few years?

Woman: Yes he did. He was very good at his job and he got pay rises and promotions – and bonuses.

Expert: And how was your lifestyle?

Woman: We had a good life. We went to Rome, Rio, Las Vegas, we extended the house and we built a swimming pool.

Expert: And each time your husband got a bonus, how much did you save for your future?

Woman: Pardon?

Expert: How much did you save for your future?

Woman: We didn't save. We borrowed more – because he was making so much.

Here is what's strange: it never occurred to this couple that:

a) while he was making huge money, it might have been a good idea to save some

b) they had created this situation, or

c) no job is forever.

In a Nutshell
A loan is money you don't have.
Be careful how you spend it.

If I had another £5,000 I would be happy!

Fred says, "If I had another £5,000 I would be happy!" and by a stroke of luck, Fred's uncle dies and leaves him 20 grand.

"Yippee!" Fred calls his wife Mary with the good news, "Hey Mary, now I can get my dream car!" Mary dissolves into tears, "But you promised me a new kitchen!" Suddenly the Fred that was going to be really happy with £5,000 is having a £20,000 argument. Mary is also unhappy!

The only solution is to get the car and the kitchen! The bill comes to £25,000 so they blow the entire inheritance and spread the extra £5,000 over their seven credit cards. Fred mumbles, "If only I had another £10,000 I'd be happy!"

The issue is not money, it's behaviour. We believe one thing but reality is totally different. There are three problems here:

- Fred thinks that money is the solution. In fact, Fred is so used to being broke that the minute he gets the money he spends it.
- We are not very skilled at figuring out what will really make us happy. In this instance, Fred is thrilled with his new car for about ten days and then everything is back to normal – except he has a large debt!
- Most of us are a lot like Fred!

We adapt very quickly to more money. We get a £500 monthly pay rise and we are delighted with the first pay cheque, satisfied with the second week and by week three we are wondering, "How long until the next spike?" We get more, we spend more, we want more.

Just because you have it, you don't have to spend it.

Joe won £200 at the races. He was so excited, he bought drinks for everyone at the bar. The bill was £300!

Michael and Lyn got married with no savings. A relative gave them £1,000 as a wedding present – it was the first chunk of money they ever had. Their friends all said, "That's fantastic! Blow it on your honeymoon!"

Clive and Louise owe £100,000 on their home and they are expecting a third child. They were skimping on groceries when suddenly they inherited £100,000 from her Dad. They bought two luxury cars and took an overseas trip. It took Dad 30 years to save it and took the kids three weeks to spend it. They still skimp on groceries.

If unexpected money comes your way, you don't have to blow it all! Sure, celebrate. But save some, eliminate some debt. If you want to be happy in hard times, it helps to plan a little.

We've probably all heard that if, at age 15 you begin saving £10 a day, you'll be a millionaire by 45. Of course the question is, "How much will a million pounds be worth by then?" Answer: "A million pounds more than if you don't do it."

Joe, Carmen, Frank and Maria's Story

Julie and I have some dear friends – Joe and Carmen, Frank and Maria. The two couples have been friends and business partners for years.

In 2000 they owned and operated a 100 room motel and restaurant. After 30 years of working mostly 7 days a week, they decided to retire. They appointed managers to operate the motel and managers to run the restaurant. Joe and Carmen built their dream home and Frank and Maria moved to a beachfront penthouse. It was time to enjoy the good life and enjoy their grandchildren.

Says Frank, "The bank valued the motel at 6 million dollars. We owed the bank 3 million. We were making our repayments plus a profit. The bank was happy.

"Then tourism took a dive and three things happened:
- the motel started losing money
- the restaurant started losing money
- the bank demanded 2 million dollars within two weeks.

"We didn't have 2 million and nobody wanted to buy our business. *The bank was going to sell us up. Overnight our whole world crashed.* We were desperate. We had worked so, so hard for 30 years for a comfortable retirement. We faced losing everything we had. It was the saddest time of our lives," says Frank.

Not Without a Fight

They had a meeting. They decided they weren't going down without a fight. They made the most difficult decision: the four of them would go back to work, to manage both the motel and the restaurant. The last thing they wanted to do was to leave their lovely homes but:

- Maria and Frank moved out of their beachside penthouse and into a motel room. They rented their home and gave the rent to the bank.
- Carmen and Joe moved out of their family home and into a motel room. They rented their house and gave the rent to the bank.

- They let most of their staff go except for a few part-timers – they had no choice. They did all the jobs they never had to do in the past.
- They washed the sheets, towels, blankets and bedspreads for all 100 rooms themselves.
- They cooked the breakfasts themselves.
- They made the beds.
- They vacuumed the rooms.
- They cleaned bathrooms and scrubbed toilets.
- Frank managed reception, Joe did the maintenance.
- At 5 p.m. they finished the chores in the motel, showered and dressed to start work in the restaurant. They were the chefs, waiters, waitresses and dishwashers. The wives cooked, the husbands worked behind the bar and on the floor.

Says Joe, "We started work at 5 a.m. every day and finished at midnight – 19 hours a day, seven days a week. We took no wages, we took no days off, we spent nothing on ourselves. This 'retirement' was the hardest time of our lives! It was heartbreaking. Our first day back in the restaurant there were four of us on duty – and for the entire evening we served one customer. The bills kept coming in. The bank was threatening to send us into receivership. We were distraught. Every Friday Frank would go to the bank."

Says Frank, "It was a nerve-racking experience – I never knew whether we had money to pay our bills. The bank was vicious. We never knew if they were going to sell us up or close us down.

"Gradually motel profits increased. Thanks to Carmen and Maria's cooking, the restaurant, which had been serving five or six people per night, was soon serving 30. That became 60 people and then 80 and eventually we had to turn people away.

"We saved the business and kept our homes. We have since leased the motel and the restaurant. Joe and Carmen are back in their dream house, Maria and I are back at the beach. Perhaps people think we're lucky."

In a Nutshell

The hardest bit is not in doing the work. The hardest bit is deciding to do the work!

One Thing Leads To Another

Sometimes we can be too picky. We might reject a job offer, reasoning, "It's not quite the job I want." If it's all you've got for the moment, grab it, master it, and watch it lead you from one thing to another. If you have nothing big going for you, start small.

I love the story of an immigrant called Nick, and how he got his first job in America: Nick had no money. He spoke no English, and he applied for a dishwashing job in a New York Italian restaurant. Before his interview with the boss, Nick went into the restaurant's bathroom and scrubbed it clean.

He then took a toothbrush and cleaned between every tile until the bathroom was completely spotless. By the time Nick had his interview, the boss was trying to figure out, "What's happened to the toilets?" It was Nick's way of saying, "I'm serious about washing dishes."

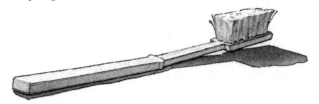

Nick got the job. A week later, the salad maker quit and Nick was on his way to becoming a chef. I think of Nick and his toothbrush when people tell me, "There are no jobs out there!" When you go looking for a job with Nick's attitude there are thousands of jobs out there. Right now, in your city. Nick is now a billionaire. Some people would say he is lucky!

A Track Record

Larry is forever trying to clinch million dollar deals. But his big deals never happen! Meanwhile his car is falling apart and even his dog is getting thin. Why? He never learned to clinch hundred dollar deals! He never developed the habit of succeeding.

You first learn to catch little fish, then big fish. Surgeons practise on tonsils before brain surgery! Most tycoons start washing cars or selling newspapers at about ten years of age. They develop a success pattern. They sharpen their skills. Then they aim higher.

What's so important about a success pattern? It's what gets you to BELIEVE IN YOURSELF. When you know in your heart that: a) "I've prepared myself for this," b) "I can do it!" and c) "I deserve it," you are on your way. When you don't believe in yourself, you are dead in the water.

Also, other people's patterns will tell you more about their future than all of their promises and all of their good intentions. If some guy wants to: a) work for you b) borrow money c) be your business partner or d) give you brain surgery, check his track record. If there's no success pattern, look out!

BRAIN SURGERY: You will need a saw, a drill and some wire or tape. STEP 1: Remove top of head ... see attached illustration of coconut..."

In a Nutshell
Wherever you are headed, take small steps; make success a habit.

Whatever it Takes

In high school biology we study the law of natural

selection. In essence it says, "Adapt or die!" If you're a tiger, you may find your lunch today at the river. Tomorrow, you may have to hunt in the forest. Tigers accept that. Humans aren't so flexible. We crawl out of bed and say, "Yesterday I got my lunch at the river. If it's not there today I'll be angry." If there's no lunch at the river for a week, we call it a depression!

You won't always find money in the same place. Your job may not always be in the same place. Sometimes the world changes your plans.

Stephen Morgan built cars for Mitsubishi until the Tonsley Park factory shut down in 2008. He says, "I was there for 22 years. It was a good job. The day that we actually closed the doors, I felt so empty." But Stephen didn't sit around feeling sorry for himself. He didn't ask, "Why me?" He became a nurse in an old folks home. His friends couldn't believe it – the macho guy becomes a carer!

Says Stephen, "They shake their heads and say, 'I can't see you doing it.' I say, 'Come and watch me.' My teenage son will ask, 'How many backsides did you wipe today, Dad?' I'll say, 'Oh, a few.' If I had a dollar for every time I was asked how many bottoms I have wiped, I'd be wealthy."

Stephen finds satisfaction helping old people: "A machine is a machine, you can fix that, but these are human beings and it takes a lot to fix a human. You get these people who are struggling and you do something simple for them. They're so happy for it! I get 50 'thank yous' a day. It's a great feeling."

Danielle Trent worked in corporate finance until she

lost her job at 30. Says Danielle, "When you get made redundant, you have a lot of things going through your head. You want to try new things but you think, Should I?... Will anyone give me an opportunity? It's easier to stay in your comfort zone. All I knew was finance. It was daunting, frightening. I really evaluated what it was I wanted to do." Danielle became an apprentice mechanic. She's loving it.

Stephen and Danielle are tigers. They adapted.

Most of us want meaning in our daily existence. Here's the catch – we discover more meaning when life is less predictable. We discover ourselves when life is less comfortable. For example, near-death experiences are uncomfortable. That's when we find out what really matters! Losing a job can be like a near death experience. Life can be richer afterwards.

Better to be a tiger than a poodle.

Mark's Story
I found a thousand books about how to be successful. What I needed was a book about surviving failure!

In the late 1970s I helped my Dad build a chain of electrical stores. He was CEO and I was his lieutenant. We started with one tiny corner shop and by the mid 1980s we had 10 stores and 70 staff – we were unstoppable! Then we hit a recession – and I discovered that "unstoppable" can also mean falling out of the sky!

As angry customers banged their fists on the windows, the liquidators marched into our stores and took the keys. We were sold up. We lost the lot – our waterfront house, the powerboat, the Mercedes – that part didn't really hurt. We also lost 70 wonderful, loyal staff. That hurt. I was ashamed and humiliated. I felt like an utter failure.

But I wasn't done yet. A year later Dad and I opened a new store and we began to claw our way back. We couldn't afford new stock so we bought the dregs and rejects that no other retailers would touch – in our industry they are called "dogs" – and we would repair them for sale. It was a long, hard road and by 2003 – after 17 years of sweat – we had three stores and 15 staff.

Then my father died, leaving my stepmother as sole director of the company. She and I couldn't agree on anything. We struggled for three years to get along – I was frustrated and she was suspicious. Then in September 2006, on the day I shook hands on the biggest business deal of my life, she used her executive power to close the company down. Without warning, in came the liquidators. We were sold up. I was absolutely gutted.

Going down for the second time, I pretended to be strong. I told my family, "We'll make it through." But I had nothing left. I had let down my employees and let down my family – again. I owed money to a lot of angry people.

> "Without warning, in came the liquidators. We were sold up. I was absolutely gutted."

Rock Bottom

I remember the night I broke. My wife and I had attended a marriage enrichment course. Driving home from this class that was designed to give us a more joyous and beautiful life, we had a massive shouting match! Alone and defeated, I staggered into the forest behind our house in the dark of night and wept bitterly for four hours. I was grieving for my father. I was grieving for 35 years of work with nothing to show for it.

I hit rock bottom. I began to ask myself important questions – not unusual questions – but when you are stripped bare, you get honest answers. I asked myself:

- Who am I?
- What really matters?
- Who really cares about me?

That was a turning point. I realised how much I loved my family and how much they loved me.

I wasn't done yet! In 2007 I saw a fresh opportunity that could erase all the pain of the previous failures. It was an ingenious advertising business and I bought a franchise. I knew it was a gamble but it looked like it would fly. Long story short – the entire franchise collapsed and I went down with it. At this moment I owe $600,000.

I'm not done yet. I've learned so much. I've discovered that I like people more than I like business. And it doesn't matter whether others think I'm a success. What matters most is that I am a decent human being.

Money doesn't buy dignity. Even if you are bankrupt

you can be honest, you can do small things well and you can keep room for hope.

I have a new direction and I am excited about the future. I now help other people deal with what I've gone through. I'm studying psychology and counseling part-time. I have written my first book *Life After Liquidation*, and I am creating a network of people to mentor and support those who have gone through business collapse.

In failure I discovered more about myself than I ever did when I was "successful."

Mark's website: www.LifeAfterLiquidation.com

Where Wealth Begins

Einstein said, "Imagination is more important than knowledge." This also applies to making money.

Let's say that you are already working for a boss but you want to make money in your spare time. You ask yourself, "What skills have I got – or what do I love to do – that people will pay me to do?" You imagine yourself making personalised greeting cards or walking the neighbours' dogs. You imagine yourself renovating your apartment or teaching aerobics. You try some ideas. Eventually one works. Where did it all begin? In your imagination.

If you already have your own business, increased profits will likely depend on how imaginatively you answer questions like...

• How can I do more with less?

• How can I manage my time better?

• What do people really want – and how can I deliver it?

And guess what! Many of your ideas won't work. Fortunately, you don't need every idea to work – just one or two.

Abel Damoussi owned a boutique in Oxford Street, London. He racked his brains to figure out how he could attract more people into his store – and hit upon the crazy idea of turning his clothing store into a nightclub after hours. You might well ask, "Who wants to boogie in a boutique?"

Abel hired a DJ and told him, "Make this place rock!" Abel created one of the coolest nightspots in the UK. When revellers wanted to buy a suit at midnight, they were told, "Not for sale! Come back when we're open." And come back they did, in droves. Business tripled. Soon Abel was turning over £20 million per year.

You say, "I'm not Abel." The principle still holds – your financial recovery and future wealth start in your imagination. Nowhere else. It is not just working harder that will make you more money – it is an increase in the quantity and the quality of your ideas.

In a Nutshell
Money is first made in your mind. If you can't see it in your mind, you'll never see it in your wallet.

Self Worth and Net Worth

Don't confuse self worth with net worth. There will always be people richer than you. There are people who are worth £50 million and they are miserable. The trouble with having 50 million is that you get to meet people who have 500 million. Then, if you measure yourself by your money, you feel like a loser.

Dean Robinson is secondary schoolteacher earning $50,000 a year. In his last job as a management consultant he earned a half a million dollars a year – or as he describes it, "a bucketload."

He wasn't sacked. He quit. He wanted a better life. He explains, "The corporate world means a lot of hours, a lot of travel, a lot of stress. It wasn't letting me do the things I wanted to do with my family." He asked himself the financial question, "Do I do this one more year or do I spend ten years teaching?" He chose the ten years.

Says Dean, "The school kids ask me, 'Did they fire you? Is that the only reason you're here?' They can't fathom why I would jump out of what I was doing – and the money that I was on – to be a schoolteacher."

But Dean has never regretted the decision, "I'm happier. I'm dealing with students. They're our future, they're smart, they're intelligent, they're witty, they're fun to work with, they're challenging. I get a new buzz and I learn something new every day."

I want my kids to be successful and happy!

Did you ever hear anyone say, "When I was a kid my parents were rich. They gave me everything I wanted and I never had to work. It was such a wonderful preparation for life. I am so proud of myself!" Sounds weird, doesn't it?

But you do hear people say, "My parents were poor and we went without. I got a part-time job to pay for my education. It taught me how to manage money. I learned responsibility and independence."

Why are so many parents determined to give their kids everything they want? Is it for their kids' benefit or is it for their own benefit? Maybe it's more about impressing the neighbours than educating the children. Maybe, if you have the money, it is just easier to spoil the kids.

In a Nutshell
Happy and successful children learn to fight their own battles, learn to budget and learn to deal with disappointment. It's called discovering the real world.

Treat Yourself Well
"It's a funny thing, life. If you refuse to accept anything but the best, you very often get it."
W. Somerset Maugham

You can't fool the world. You can't treat yourself badly and expect that the world is going to respect you and pay you big bucks. You can tell everyone that you are ready to live the good life, but if on a daily basis you make excuses and accept second best, your future will be more of the same.

You are always creating. Every day is important, your every thought is important. Fred says, "When I get successful, I'll quit living like a rat!" No Fred. To be a success you have to begin to live it, you have to feel it now.

Fred says, "Does that mean I should eat in all the best restaurants?" Probably not yet. But you could sit in one... and buy a coffee. Improving your quality of life is like bringing together the pieces of a jigsaw. Steadily, sensibly, you lift your sights. You stretch your thinking. You try new things, you go to new places, break out of old habits.

Then you look back in a year or two and say, "Wow. How far I've come!"

Prosperity Checklist

With prosperity there is no one trick or gimmick. You need to do what wealthy people do, which includes most of the following:

- Quit telling yourself and other people that you are broke. Tell yourself every day, "I'm prosperous." What you think is what you get.
- Believe in your heart and soul that you have the same right to a rich life as anyone else.

- Study wealth! Find out how wealthy people operate.
- Develop your skills and expand your knowledge.
- Spend time with motivated people.
- Detach from results. If you are applying for a job or doing a deal, let go.
- Start saving 10% of your income. Every week, before you spend one penny, make that deposit.
- Nurture yourself: clean up your house, your wardrobe, your car – throw out the junk. If you have clothes that make you feel like a loser, ditch them.
  You need to feel good.
- Give your best shot to whatever is in front of you, however small, and opportunity will begin to find you.
- Start anywhere you can.
- Be grateful – for however little you have right now. Gratitude keeps good things coming.

That's enough.

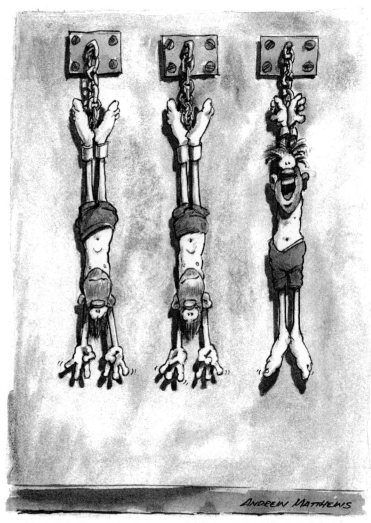

+ *"Sometimes I ask myself: 'Why am I the lucky one?'"*

8

Breakthroughs

Imagine you are driving a race car at 150 miles an hour when suddenly you find yourself sliding out of control and heading for a brick wall. What do you do?

If you said, "Close my eyes" that's not a good answer.

Here's what all race car drivers know and what Toyota Corolla drivers should know – when you lose control, you keep your eyes fixed on *where you want to go*. You don't look at where you have been. You don't even look at where you are. You focus on *where you need to get to*.

So what about when your life veers out of control? The same rule applies. You keep your eyes fixed on where you want to go. If you have just lost all your money, you don't look back. If you just lost your job, you don't look back. If you just left a relationship, you don't look back. You forget about blaming your boyfriend. You forget about blaming yourself.

You hold in your mind what you want. You hold in your mind WHERE YOU WANT TO GO.

Focus on What You Want

The principle of focus *on where you want to go* applies to everything you do. It is also supported by scientific research. Before you do anything in your life, you must first see it in your mind. Before you can swing a golf club, you picture it in your imagination. To grab a drink from the refrigerator, you *visualise* the action – very briefly – in your mind. If you don't picture it, it doesn't happen.

Let's explore visualisation a little further. Let's say we stuck a dozen electrodes to your scalp and connected you by some long wires to an electroencephalograph to measure your brain activity. We then got another very large wire and strung it above Niagara Falls so we could monitor your thoughts while you did a spot of tightrope walking.

Assuming you returned safely, let's say you then sat down in a chair and vividly *imagined* yourself strolling across Niagara Falls. You would demonstrate something very interesting about brain activity. The exact *same areas* of your brain are activated whether you are *actually tightrope walking* or *imagining it.*

Your brain cannot tell the difference between a real and a vividly imagined experience. When you *mentally rehearse*, your brain cells undergo electrochemical changes, the same as if you were actually skating, dancing, putting or panicking.

What does this mean?

- That when you visualise you program your brain.
- That when you imagine yourself performing perfectly, you train your brain for peak performance.

You might say, "But this information has been around since the 1950s!" Correct. There's not an elite golfer, singer, public speaker, race car driver or cat burglar who doesn't use visualisation. But the rest of us often underestimate the power of mental rehearsal.

Why do children learn so fast? They naturally use visualisation, they play imaginary mental movies. Your two-year-old doesn't need to read this chapter.

For her, mental rehearsal is automatic. The problem is this: playing mental movies is not very sophisticated or intellectual. So if we are adults, or if we are *sophisticated or intellectual* we might dismiss this kind of critical information.

If you want to change any habit, if you want to be more punctual, more organised, more confident or even happier, you need to picture it – vividly, repeatedly. Over weeks and months you'll notice the transformation. Too easy? This is not a *once or twice* thing. Make it a daily routine.

In a Nutshell
You don't achieve great things by looking at *what you are*. You achieve great things by looking at *what you want to be* – and then playing those movies in your mind.

Creating Results

You can replace old habits by playing mental movies, but expect some resistance. Your old self will try to hang on – but you can overwrite it. No one has to stay stuck.

Many people use their mind "backwards" – in other words, they dwell on what they *don't want* – and then wonder why they get bad results. To explain: If I say to you, "Don't think of a blue kangaroo," what do you think of? So what would happen if you were planning to give a speech to a hundred people, and you kept telling yourself, "Don't be nervous! Don't forget your lines!" You would screw it up – and then ask yourself, "Why did this happen when I told myself NOT to be an idiot?"

When you tell yourself, "Don't be nervous! Don't shake!", you get mental pictures of you shaking and stammering. These images filter into your subconscious and program your brain for a shaking, stammering performance! So you shake and stammer. It's the law of the mind. No other result is possible.

To give a confident speech, you need a picture in your head of you giving a great speech *before you even stand up.* Here's the critical thing that sabotages countless lives: here's what every parent should know and what every teacher should teach: here's what should be written across the sky in letters 1,000 feet tall:

*YOU CANNOT GIVE YOUR MIND A MESSAGE **NOT** TO DO SOMETHING. YOUR SUBCONSCIOUS MIND NEEDS A PICTURE OF **WHAT YOU WANT**.*

If you spend your whole life saying:

- I don't want to be lonely
- I don't want to be fat, or
- I don't want to be broke

you imprint your mind with pictures of what you *don't want* – loneliness, fatness, brokeness – and that is what you get. That is all that your mind can deliver. *Think about something YOU WANT and YOU MOVE TOWARD IT. Think about something YOU DON'T WANT and YOU MOVE TOWARD IT.*

Your subconscious mind doesn't understand "No." It doesn't understand "I don't want!"

This explains why confidence is so critical. When you are confident, you have only positive pictures in your mind – of a relaxed job interview, of a successful driving test, of a great piano recital. When you are confident, you don't play disaster movies, you play success movies – so you regularly succeed. You're not perfect, but you always give yourself the best possible chance.

For your memory to work, you focus on what you want. How often have you said to yourself, "I MUSTN'T FORGET my diary, phone, passport," and then left it in the taxi? Your mind cannot move away from forgetting. When you tell yourself "I don't want to forget my book," you are halfway toward spending the day without it.

Positive thinking works because positive thinkers have the habit of picturing what they want, not what they fear! What you think is what you get.

What we tell others

Imagine you are a basketball coach. Your team is in the final and the game is a heart-stopper – you're one point down with two seconds left on the clock, your forward has the ball and he's shooting for glory. You stand up and shout at the top of your lungs, "Don't miss it!"

Would that help? It wouldn't! He needs a picture in his mind of *what he wants*.

Frustrated parents constantly tell their children what they *don't want them to do!* "Don't scream. Don't smash grandma's Ming vase. Don't fall out of that tree." When you tell your ten-year-old, "Don't break your leg," you are actually helping to set him up for a stay in hospital.

What should you say? "Hold on. Climb safely."

In a Nutshell

Whatever you want, picture it in your mind. The more you picture it, the easier it is to do it. You can change. You're a human being – you're not a tree.

I'm Stuck in this Job

Did you ever ask yourself, "What am I doing in this stupid job?" Do you ever feel as if you are stuck? If you feel frustrated or unhappy at work – whether you're a chicken plucker or a brain surgeon – your best strategy is: GIVE IT ALL YOU'VE GOT.

Why? When you give it all you've got you feel better about yourself. Your success in life is much more to do with *how you feel* than *what you know*. The only way to feel good in your job is to do it as well as you can.

**"The company has decided to recognise
your contribution!"**

Also, when you give your all:
- You develop your skills.
- You develop a reputation.
- Sometime, someone will notice you and offer you
a better position, or:
- You'll get the confidence to go do your own thing.

When you are focused and enthusiastic, you are
a magnet for new opportunity because happy and
enthusiastic people attract other happy and enthusiastic
people. Fred says, "If I had a great job, I would really
work hard – but I've got this lousy job so I just sleep all
day!" No, Fred! When we continually give our best, life
leads us toward new opportunities. Sometimes it takes
a while, but it happens.

One more thing: opportunities, job offers – and
romance – usually arrive when we least expect them.
Breakthroughs mostly happen in the most unlikely
situations. It's life's way of reminding us to respect

everyone we meet. It's also life's way of reminding us to keep an open mind.

In a Nutshell
Successful people tell themselves, "If I make the most of this opportunity, I'll get a bigger one."

Commitment

"When someone makes a decision, he is really diving into a strong current that will carry him to places he had never dreamed of when he first made the decision." Paulo Coelho

We can learn a lot from ANTS! Find an ant that's going about his business, and put a brick in his way! What will he do? He'll try getting under it, he'll try getting over it, he'll try going through it. How long will he try? Until he dies! Isn't that a powerful mindset: *Try until you die!*

Most people QUIT! Whether it's aerobics or piano lessons or life insurance, they quit. And this is great news. It means that if you want to get to the very top in your field, you don't even have to be very bright. If you just hang around long enough, everyone else will leave!

The mountain climber who conquers Everest is the one who says, "I will do it." The guy who says, "I'll give it my best shot" or "I'll try" will likely come home early. The same goes for the salesman, the marathon runner or the boyfriend. To get results you have to get serious. Life rewards effort, not excuses.

Moya's Story

Old men would bring me their smelly, urine-stained trousers to have the corroded zips replaced. The stench was so sickening I would be on the verge of throwing up, and asking myself, "How did my life get to this?"

I had read about people going "bankrupt" but I never knew what it meant, and anyway, I figured it could never happen to me...

Before I was born my father bought a millionaire's holiday shack. It was a spectacular property and a real landmark, smack in the middle of town on a huge chunk of land, surrounded by beaches on three sides. Dad transformed this house into the Peninsula Hotel, with bars, a nightclub and hotel rooms.

To me as a child, the hotel was simply "home," a piece of paradise with endless room to play. I was the youngest of three children. We swam off the pier, we rowed about in boats and we caught prawns, crabs and all kinds of fish.

If You Can't Beat Them, Join Them

Growing up I was surrounded by alcohol. Drinking was normal and being drunk was supposed to mean "being happy." Everyone at the hotel drank: my father drank, my parent's friends all drank and my mother was an alcoholic. Mum would finish a bottle of sherry every night. The more my mother drank, the more I craved her attention.

When my first marriage broke up, I began to drink to drown my loneliness and I soon became an ugly alcoholic. When I wasn't working I was drinking, and my children suffered. Hopelessly depressed, I tried to kill myself with pills. I tried to drown myself in a river. Even when I married my second husband, Rob, I was out of control – he was violent but I was worse!

Losing Everything

With 50 years of effort, Dad had steadily built the business. I loved working in the hotel, I was proud to be a part of it and felt secure that the hotel would always be there – and so would we.

In 1982 he handed over the management to us three children. It was debt free and providing for us all. We were set for life.

By 1993 we were bankrupt. How does a thriving family business go broke? It doesn't matter now who was to blame but this was our excuse:

- too many managers on outrageous salaries
- too many employees doing too little work
- too much money wasted on renovations, and
- no stock control.

And it didn't help that I was constantly drunk!

Suddenly one Friday evening, the bank sent in the receivers – eight men with walkie-talkies arrived, swarming into the hotel like a SWAT team, through the bars and into the kitchen, restaurant and storerooms. We watched in helpless disbelief. It was heartbreaking and embarrassing. They demanded the keys to the front door and the safe. From then on we were never left alone in the hotel until everything was sold up.

When we lost the hotel, Rob and I lost our home plus another business we owned – a childrenswear store. My car was towed away. The bailiff came to visit me asking if I had any jewellery to declare – and I remember frantically trying to turn my engagement ring around. I was sick with shame.

> "We sold our dining room suite to pay the bills and we ate on the floor."

Though we had no credit references, we managed to rent a small house. We were allowed to keep some very basic furniture: Rob got to keep his tools and I kept my sewing machine. When you live in a small town, there's no escaping. People would call us looking for money but we had nothing left. We also had three children to feed.

Inch by Inch
We sold our dining room suite to pay bills and we ate on the floor:
- Rob went to work laying bricks
- I delivered dry-cleaning all over town for five dollars an hour

- I cleaned the local laundromat four times a day, and
- the kids and I delivered newspapers.

Being a dressmaker, I began sewing. I would sew anything. Old men would bring me their smelly, urine-stained trousers to have the corroded zips replaced. The stench was so sickening I would be on the verge of throwing up, and asking myself, "How did my life get to this?"

Inch by inch we took control of our lives. We pulled together as a family like we never had before:

- we set goals
- we made lists of chores and shared them out
- we did a family budget, and
- I quit drinking alcohol.

As a bankrupt I couldn't borrow money so I did a deal with my sister-in-law, Diane, to buy her car and slowly pay her back. I learned to take responsibility. For example, when I couldn't pay the electricity bill, instead of ignoring it, I would call the company and we would work out a payment schedule of, say $20 a week.

Diane was in multilevel marketing, selling Nutrimetics cosmetics. Though I am a shy person, I thought, "I can probably do that." I borrowed the money to buy the starter kit and off I went downtown to distribute my pamphlets. I went from store to store. I talked to people on the street. My plan was to get people to agree to hold a "party" in their home where I could sell my lipsticks.

By the end of day one I had 12 parties organised. I was petrified as to how I would ever manage to stand up and speak at these events – but I was on my way.

I found customers by going through the phone book and calling strangers. I worked seven days a week and did five or more shows per week. Every time I gave out a brochure, I followed up. Every time I promised, I delivered. Some nights I would drive four hours to give a presentation to have no one show up! But my *Nutrimetics* friends gave me support and inspiration. Month by month my sales increased and I began to feel a sense of accomplishment I had never felt before.

My sales performance qualified me for overseas vacations to America and Malaysia – and I got to take my husband Rob. In Hawaii I told my story onstage to an audience of 2,000 people; how proud I felt. As a bankrupt, my passport had been confiscated – so each time I won an overseas trip, I had to re-apply for my passport – and give it back to the authorities on my return. Nobody on those trips could have understood my strange mix of emotions – feeling exhilarated at the conference and humiliated on my return.

The long days and late nights paid off. I became a sales director in the company and over the next seven years earned three company cars.

At 46 I was ready for a new challenge and I decided to try selling real estate. I knew nothing about real estate and I failed the course on my first attempt. But I persevered, got my licence, and in my first year was fortunate to win the company's state-wide award for rookie of the year. Real estate has been rewarding and Rob and I continue to work hard.

Mistakes

I have made more stupid mistakes than most people:

- I was a bad mother and wife
- I was depressed
- I was bankrupt
- I was an alcoholic, and
- I tried to kill myself a few times.

Today I count my blessings. Losing the family business forced me to grow in ways I never imagined. I have been loved by a wonderful man for 28 years. Despite a shaky start, we are a close, loving family and I have three beautiful grandchildren. We now have a nice home near the beach and we have bought several investment properties.

> *"It is 19 years since I drank alcohol."*

Today I am happy and at peace with myself. Today we have enough to live a good life. It beats being bankrupt. *It is 19 years since I drank alcohol.* We have overcome hard times.

Moya's website:
www.inspirational-quotes-and-thoughts.com

But I Can't Change

People say, "But I can't change. It's just the way I am." Success is not about intelligence, it's more about resolve. When you're broke you do things that you would never try if you were comfortable.

Says Moya:

- "I wrote down my life goals – it gave me something to hope for."
- "I listed my tasks each day and did the toughest jobs first – it's how I beat procrastination."
- "I lived one day at a time – somehow, when you focus on the job at hand, everything else seems to sort itself out."
- "I was committed. I just did whatever it took." Wherever you are, you can do the same.

Dianne's Story

My religious Dad warned me about the thug with the loud car that lived across the street. He said, "Don't you ever get involved with That!" But "That" started following me home from work. Then one day I got into his car. We went out. By 16 I was pregnant and married.

His name was Richard. He hit me throughout the pregnancy. Sometimes I would fight back. One night I knocked him unconscious. Despite the assaults, our first son Terry was born healthy. Not so our second son, Heath, who was born six years later with hydrocephalus (fluid on the brain) and other abnormalities.

Heath was not expected to live. He needed physiotherapy and suction every three hours. He slept in a special chair – the doctors warned me that if he lay flat he would die. At night Richard would get drunk, beat me up, throw me out of the house and take baby Heath into bed with him. I would be desperate. I would wait until Richard was asleep, sneak back into the house and retrieve Heath. It was a living nightmare!

My son Terry was good-looking, athletic and popular. Everything came easy to Terry. Heath was the compassionate one, wise beyond his years. Miraculously, after the first nerve-wracking year of his life, Heath was quite healthy. After seven years of hell I divorced Richard and life with my boys was wonderful.

Then at 12, Heath began to get very sick. One moment he would be in the weight-lifting championships or the BMX state titles – and within 12 hours he would be having major brain surgery. The operations were never-ending. Heath spent most of his teen years in hospital.

Terry was a good boy but he tended to follow the crowd. He started drinking at 14, was into dope by 16, and then hard drugs. I would find him in the gutter, unwashed, having worn the same clothes for a week. I would buy him new clothes, he'd take a bath, I would feed him and we would go to visit Heath in hospital. Then Terry would disappear. A week later I would find him in a similar gutter and we would do the same thing all over again.

Heath knew that he could die anytime and so did I. For three years I virtually lived at the hospital.

Heath decided very early on that he wanted to donate his organs to help other sick kids. He said, "Let them take whatever but leave my brain alone – it's had enough." We signed the forms and at the top we wrote in large letters, "Leave Brain Intact." By age 16 Heath became very ill with strokes and infections and finally, 20 days before his 17th birthday, he died in his bed with me sitting beside him.

I cried my heart out. I felt such indescribable loss but I tried to focus on positives. I remember thinking at the funeral, "At least he has his brain."

And then the bombshell: I found out through the funeral director that the hospital had taken his brain. That was the last straw! How dare they! I felt so angry, abused, manipulated. I felt that I had let my boy down and I went into deep depression.

Enough is Enough

I had a stockpile of Heath's drugs and I tried to kill myself. I took about 30 pills but as fate would have it, a friend phoned me just after I'd swallowed the tablets. She thought I sounded weird and called a friend that lived close by. I was taken to the hospital by ambulance. I survived but I didn't want to be alive.

We do strange things whilst grieving. I would drive to the hospital just to walk through the wards, looking for Heath. I knew he was dead but still I went, just to make sure he wasn't there.

I was still depressed from Heath's death when my ex-husband, Richard, fell off a bar stool and died – literally.

He had a heart attack. Terry came from interstate for the funeral – by now Terry was 26, he had a steady girlfriend, a son, and another one on the way. The day after the funeral a local policeman arrived at my front door.

He said, "Bad news. He's dead."

I said, "I know Richard is dead."

The policeman said, "No, TERRY is dead."

I said, "Terry is not dead. His *father* died."

The policeman insisted on taking me to the hospital where I found a group of Terry's friends in tears. Terry had been found in a toilet in the Argyle Mall. He had injected heroin and had a massive heart attack.

My boys were my life. I felt so cheated, in fact, doubly cheated. I had married an alcoholic who bashed us. I had one sick son and one healthy son. I buried them both. I felt cursed. I would tell myself, "Thank God I don't have any more children. I would be waiting for them to die." I felt like I didn't deserve to be alive. I wasn't guilty; I couldn't have done any more. I was angry and heartbroken; I felt hopeless.

I have little recollection of the third time I attempted suicide. The police found me in a churchyard, battered and bloody. My teeth had been knocked out and I was banging my head against a wall. My car was close by, the motor was running and my headlights were on. The police thought that I had been attacked. I have no idea how I got there but I wasn't attacked. I had done it myself. I spent the next week in a psychiatric ward and they let me out on Christmas Eve.

I felt like I had been climbing a mountain for years, and each time I almost reached the top, somebody or something would push me off again. In deep depression, everything is a huge effort: even getting dressed is an almost impossible task. I would be managing okay and then I would hear a song, or see a boy of Heath's age, or I would pass a car like the one Terry drove, and I would slide back into that dark tunnel.

For years I spent my free time at the cemetery, planting flowers and talking to my boys. That was part of my healing.

It does get easier. At first it's a physical pain like someone is crushing your heart – it really hurts. Gradually you learn how to live without a loved one. You find a life; like being a baby again, you learn how to walk, how to talk, how to laugh.

Slowly I began to mend. Slowly I began to like myself and feel human. I began to feel I had a right to be alive, instead of just being the mother of those two dead kids.

> "At first it's a physical pain like someone is crushing your heart – it really hurts. Gradually you learn how to live without a loved one."

These days I remember the good times. I know I was a good mother. I couldn't have done more for my boys. I have no partner. I am alone but not lonely. I am at peace now. I am happier – and I am able to enjoy quality time with my grandsons.

Dianne's email address: dmmulc@hotmail.com

"I know my husband can be loving and kind – he's that way with the dog!"

9

Gratitude

"If the only prayer you say in your whole life is 'Thank you,' that would suffice."
Meister Eckhart

What is the main difference between happy people and unhappy people? Happy people focus on what they have. Unhappy focus on what's missing.

If you get up every morning and look for faults, you will find them:

- in your wife – "She's put on weight"
- in your kids – "They're ungrateful"
- your car – "My neighbour drives a Porsche!"
- your job – "The boss is an idiot."

You can send yourself into a descending spiral.

If every morning you look for reasons to feel good, you'll find them:

- with your wife – "She is always bright and she is always there for me"
- your car – "It's old but it's paid for"
- your job – "It's great to have one!"

As you develop the daily habit of looking for good things, your life will steadily improve. When you are happy, life begins to support you. *Decide* to be happy with the world as it is. Be happy with what you have. Look for good things in other people. Celebrate others' success and happiness.

If someone is causing you grief – if your wife is fat and lazy, *you don't pretend* that she is slim and energetic –

but *you do* continue to look for her other qualities. As you do so, she will change – or her laziness will become a lesser part of your experience.

If you are underpaid in your job, you don't try to convince yourself that you are *well paid* – but you look for good things in your job. As you start to feel better about your job, so you will attract more opportunities within your job – or perhaps another job.

Every time you see someone living the kind of life that you would like, tell yourself, "Here's more evidence that good things are possible!" When you see someone who is making easy money, tell yourself, "Wonderful! There's more evidence that all this is possible for me too!"

If you want to be grateful, you wake up grateful. If you say, "*When my life gets better, then I'll be grateful,*" you never will be! Start where you are.

In a nutshell
Every time you say a silent "Thank you" you become more peaceful – and more powerful.

Why listen to your mother when you can learn the hard way?

My mother tried to teach me about gratitude. I remember as a ten-year-old being reminded that I should be grateful for all the good things I had in my life… "Say grace, say prayers, be thankful for loving parents, plenty of food, a warm bed, brothers and sisters and all the other things you take for granted."

I remember times when I was complaining that the world was rotten and everything stinks, Mum would give me homework. She would send me to my bedroom with pencil and paper to make a list of all the things for which I was grateful! Of course, I never wrote anything. And I saw no value in the exercise. If God happened to exist, there seemed no point in giving him the attention that I could be giving my tennis game.

Years later I still hadn't got the message, but fortunately Mum never quit on me.

In the 1980s I began a seminar business. It was a weekend course focused on relaxation, goal setting and success. It was a franchise business and I acquired the rights for my city. My friend Paul started the same business in Sydney at the same time. In fact we both conducted our very first seminar on exactly the same weekend in May 1985.

In my first seminar, I had 14 students and Paul also had 14. Fourteen students just covered costs. It seemed like a good start. I was happy. A month later we both held our second seminar. I had 12 students and Paul had 35. The next month, I had 11 and he had 60. The following month, I had ten and he had 100.

It is embarrassing teaching seminars about *being successful* when you are going broke. I became dissatisfied with everything. I blamed my city, I blamed my advertising programme, I blamed the weather, I blamed the stupid people who didn't do my course and the stupid people who did. I also blamed myself – but that didn't help either.

Then my Mum gave me the same advice she gave me when I was ten. She said, "Concentrate on what you have. Be thankful for the people you have." And she probably mentioned the Bible.

Frustrated and left with no one else to blame, I quit wishing I was Paul. I quit wishing I had his business. I decided to be happy with what I had. I did my best with what I had. My next seminar had 30 people. The following had 55. Things began to turn around. That painful six months was a serious lesson in gratitude.

A Common Message

Jesus, Buddha, Mohammed and others taught that we should count our blessings. They taught, "What you think is important! Be grateful!" They recommended gratitude for very practical reasons.

So, you say, "How exactly does this gratitude thing work?"

Here's my explanation: the most enlightened beings amongst us suggest that the world is actually perfect. They suggest that when we are suffering, the problem is not with the world but with our thinking. Most of us would agree with this to some extent.

When we are critical of everything and everybody, we are out of harmony. Life is a struggle and we feel like we're always in the wrong place at the wrong time.

When we see the world as perfect – that is, when we are feeling deep gratitude – we are in harmony with everything. When we are in harmony, life flows, opportunities arise, we are relaxed and happy.

When you are grateful for what you DO HAVE, your

predominant thought is, "Good things keep on coming," so that will be your experience. When you wake up every day feeling thankful for another meal, another 24 hours with your family, you are reaffirming that you have a joyful life surrounded by people you care about. As you focus on the richness of your life so it will continue.

We give thanks for OUR benefit.

When I met my wife Julie, I noticed that for all her beautiful qualities, she has one shortcoming. She can't add up! But although she is never quite sure what she has earned, what she is owed and what she has spent, she has always enjoyed prosperity. She spends big and she believes in abundance. Julie is a living demonstration that, as far as quality of life is concerned, *a sense of gratitude, and an inner knowing that life will bless you,* are more important than logic and mathematics.

The universe is essentially fairly forgiving, but if you consistently concentrate on what you don't have, you will get less and less of what you want.

The people who enjoy the most beautiful relationships are the people who value them highly. The people who lead active and fulfilling lives are the people who are consistently rejoicing in what life delivers.

In a Nutshell
An attitude of gratitude ensures that our attention is on what we want. It is an excellent system, really. What if the reverse were true and the more we grizzled and moaned, the more we got?

Thank You, Julie

This is a good time for me to say, "Thank you, Julie."

Julie has been my publisher for 15 years. She previously ran an advertising agency, had an interior decoration business and more recently owned and operated a finishing and modelling school – all very successful and entirely without my help!

She gave up a blossoming career that she really loved to take our books around the world.

Why would you ever want to become a publisher? The author gets all the credit, the publisher does all the hard work and gets no credit and no thanks! When you are the wife of the author, it's even worse!

The background to *Happiness in Hard Times* is this:

• Julie had the idea for this book and chose the title

• Julie had the brainwave to include all the stories

• Julie stayed up late at night interviewing all the contributors – and kept in touch with everybody by phone and email

• we wrote this book together – then Julie did the editing, and

• Julie now gets to lose more sleep as she takes *Happiness in Hard Times* around the world.

Julie always seems to know what to do. When I didn't know where to start, Julie knew. When I didn't know where the book was going, Julie knew, always. If *Happiness in Hard Times* has touched you, please don't email me. Let Julie know. This book happened because of Julie's vision and determination. Thank you my darling.

Craig's Story

My stepdad kicked Mum, my two sisters and me out of the house when I was 12. We left with nothing but our clothes and lived in a caravan. We tried going back once, only to be thrown out again. As a child, I never felt good enough.

As a teenager I was awkward and insecure. I had panic attacks, I let people walk all over me. Alcohol numbed the pain and gave me some confidence. I began to mix with a "cool" crowd in bars and nightclubs – I felt like part of a "family." We did drugs like cocaine, ecstasy, marijuana and LSD.

Then my dearest friend, Anthony, was diagnosed with HIV. I knew little about the disease but decided to have a check-up, just in case. That is when the doctor told me, "You've got HIV. You've got five or ten years to live. Go live your life." I was 19 – and stunned! But I remember walking out of that hospital and saying to myself, this HIV isn't going to get me... EVER."

Anthony was HIV positive for four years before developing AIDS – and he survived just two years after that. For the last three months I helped care for him. It broke my heart and I still miss him.

My Greatest Teacher

HIV shocked me to my senses and I began to look inside myself. I got enormous help from Louise Hay's book *You Can Heal Your Life*. I learned to use positive affirmations. I quit taking life – and myself – so seriously.

My family had seen Anthony go through hell, and I

didn't want them to worry so I didn't tell my family until about ten years into my diagnosis. They were

"HIV is the best thing that could have happened to me."

devastated but very supportive, and they still are.

Learning to love myself and choosing to forgive other people changed my life. Nowadays, I feel comfortable in my own skin, I have self-confidence and I don't take crap. I enjoy the simple things in life. I like who I am. When you like who you are, you are happy.

I've been HIV positive for 24 years now. HIV is the best thing that could have happened to me. I was self-destructing. If I hadn't contracted HIV, I would have ended up dead in some gutter.

My Mum is now in stage three of asbestos cancer (mesothelioma). She was diagnosed six years ago and given 12 months to live. She's still going. Mum always told me, "God gives us nothing we can't handle."

I am now studying to help others in similar situations to my own. My philosophy is:

- take nothing for granted
- giving is more important than receiving
- anything is possible.

HIV has been my greatest teacher and blessing.

Craig's email: positive_times@hotmail.com

"I can't help it – I come from a family of worriers!"

10

Let Go!

The Buddhists talk about attachment. You know about it. When we chase girlfriends, boyfriends – even dogs – they run away! Why? Because we are chasing them! When we try to trap people in relationships, they can't wait to escape! When we LET GO, they often come back!

Did you ever spend weeks searching for an apartment but found nothing fit for human habitation? After endless frustration you quit – and that's when you found it. As soon as you signed the lease, you discovered three more perfect apartments without even looking!

Were you ever desperate for work but nobody needed you – until you found a job, and then everybody wanted you! Or did you ever want to sell something – a stroller, a laptop, a parachute? Nobody wanted it so you gave it away. When you no longer had it, everyone wanted to buy it. How often do you hear of childless couples that adopt – and then, within months, the wife falls pregnant? What is going on here?

When we can't find a job or an apartment, we start to have desperation thoughts. We become focused on what we *don't have*. When our thoughts are, "Oh no, I have no place to live," we get more of the same – *no place to live*.

When our thoughts are, "Oh no, I can't get a job, a boyfriend, a plane ticket," our thoughts are on what we *lack* – so we continue creating and attracting the same experience – lack.

Once we get the job, the boyfriend, the apartment, our thinking shifts from, "I *need* this" to "I *have* what I need." "I *have* what I need" is a totally different thought vibration. "I *have* what I need" is your most powerful state. "I *have* what I need" is the mindset for a much easier life!

Fred says, "But you don't get it! I don't *have* what I need! When I *have* what I need, then I'll be happy." Perfectly understandable, Fred, but the results of this approach are always disappointing.

Don't take my word for it. Spend a month telling yourself at every opportunity, "I have everything I need." Spend a month telling yourself, "My life is unfolding perfectly." More and more you will find your life working out. Don't worry about figuring it out. Just keep doing what works.

In a Nutshell
The trick to the game of life is to feel happy, grateful and content first.

Detachment

Detachment is not disinterest. It is possible to be detached and still be very determined. People who are detached and determined know that *effort and excellence are ultimately rewarded.* They say, *"If I don't win this time, I'll win the next time, or the time after that."*

Let's say you apply for a job at Loony Larry's Computers. You are excited about the opportunity and you prepare carefully. You write out your interview speech and you practise it in front of the bathroom mirror. You even get new shoes and a haircut. You arrive early for the interview and you give it your best shot.

What next? You go home and you get on with your life. You enrol in extra study. You plan your next job application. If you get hired by Loony Larry, you're happy. If not, you are still moving forward.

Disinterested people say, "Who cares and why bother?" Desperate people say, "If I don't get this I'll die!" When you are determined and detached, you say, "One way or another, I will get a good job – and I don't care how long it takes."

In a Nutshell
Nature doesn't understand desperation!
Nature seeks balance, and you can't be desperate *and* balanced. Life doesn't have to be an endless struggle.
Let things flow. This is not indifference; it's not forcing things.
There's such a thing as trying too hard!

Attracting Opportunity

You met Caroline in Chapter 2. Caroline has spent the last 40 years managing hotels all over the world – island resorts on the Great Barrier Reef, hotels in the Himalayas and northern Thailand, properties on Sydney Harbour.

Now here's what's curious:
- she has no training in hospitality or hotel management, and

• she has never once formally applied for a job.

You might say, "I am getting ten bucks an hour flipping burgers and you're talking about this woman who keeps pulling these great jobs all around the world?" That's right! *This woman* has never been out of work. She has had 14 management positions in 40 years, none of which she applied for. It's not luck.

Why is Caroline such a magnet for opportunity? She has absolutely no fear of being unemployed. She is totally unattached. Her experience in the workplace is different from most people's because her thinking is different from most people's.

She says, "It's crazy. I'm not even a great manager but these jobs just happen. I live in blind trust. I know that the right job will always come at the right time."

Caroline was once appointed manager of *Clear Mountain Health Retreat.* She said, "I didn't apply for it and I never even knew I had the job! I had gone to Greece for five months and while I was away, my husband David applied for the position. When he met the owners, everyone agreed that the job suited me better. When I stepped off the plane, David said, 'Lucky you came home. You start work tomorrow!'"

If you spend time in one of Caroline's hotels, here's what you notice: she loves her staff, she cherishes her guests and she lives in the moment. That's the secret: no fear and live one day at a time. When you are absorbed in the moment, life works out.

Living in the Present

What do most airline passengers do the minute they touch down? Even as the plane is hurtling across the tarmac, they begin hauling their stuff toward the exit. No matter that they will spend the next 25 minutes waiting at the baggage carousel – they are in a hurry! And because they hurry, you hurry. It's habit. And so the flight attendant announces one more time, "For your own safety please remain seated –"

We spend our lives anticipating, "Once I get this, once I become that – I should be there but I am here."

Self-help gurus tell us to *live in the present* but does it matter?

It matters. Because when you are happy, enthusiastic and absorbed you plug into the power of the universe. When you are dissatisfied, distracted, and depressed you are unplugged and on your own – and when you are on your own, you are powerless to attract anything better. Your key to a better life is to feel good *now*, not next week, not when your boyfriend finally pops the question, not when peace is declared in the Middle East.

This is all there is: moment to moment living. It is not going to get any better. Accept that and the struggle stops.

In a Nutshell
Your life will work to the extent that you can say:
- there is nothing I need other than this moment
- there is no one I need to impress and no one I need to become
- I am what I am
- I have everything I need to be happy.

Jenny's Story

I left school at 15 with no goals. When I was 22 a friend said, "Why don't you go to university?" The thought had never entered my head! I thought uni was for "rich and brainy kids"! But I enrolled and to my surprise I did well. At university I also met the love of my life: Alex.

Alex was talented, musical, interesting and

passionate. Unfortunately, two of his passions were vodka and any drug he could get hold of. Alex was verbally and physically abusive. I made excuses for him. I told myself, "He's a migrant, he had strict parents, nobody understands his artistic temperament." Alex and I had two children together: a son, Jex, and a daughter, Marli. Finally, after eight years – for my own sanity and safety – I left with my children when they were still infants.

When Jex was four months old I became concerned that he had a hearing problem. It was Chistmas Day and my uncle was playing the bagpipes. The entire family was covering its ears in agony but Jex didn't even flinch. Medical tests confirmed that he was profoundly deaf. Deafness didn't faze me; I just wanted to do what I could to help Jex communicate! We both learned sign language and by age three he was fluent. He was a busy, happy child.

> "DEAF AND BLIND? I contemplated murder-suicide. First I would take Jex, then me."

But his next diagnosis tore me apart. Jex was becoming angry and frustrated at school. At seven, I took him for testing and he was diagnosed with Usher Syndrome. The doctors said, "He will lose most, or maybe all of his vision." DEAF AND BLIND? What use was sign language now? Who would care for him?

My world collapsed. I went through all the stages of grief; denial, anger, bargaining, depression. I contemplated murder-suicide. First I would take Jex, then me.

Doctors said there was no hope to save his sight, but still we tried everything. We visited naturopaths, acupuncturists, kinaesiologists and healers, we put him on vitamin supplements.

Then another blow: confirmation that Jex had Tourette's Syndrome – the condition where people make involuntary noises and twitches. They can't help it. Jex couldn't help it – but school children don't understand. Kids can be cruel.

Looking for Positives

I would wake up at 3 a.m., petrified for Jex. "What will happen to him?" The future was crushing me. Somehow I had to force my brain to stay in the present, so:

- I began to look for positive things in my life. Each night I wrote lists of everything good that had happened to me that day.
- I repeated affirmations to keep me in the present moment.
- I exercised regularly and maintained my own social life.
- I started meditating.

Somehow I had to TRUST that Jex would be okay. I told myself, "Even with three senses Jex can have a life. He can enjoy good food and massages. Communication will be more intimate but still possible." As Jex lost more and more sight, so he adapted, and so my fears gradually diminished.

I just had to let go. When Jex started high school he lived with two extraordinary deaf guys, one also had Usher's. They became his friends, his mentors and helped us all toward acceptance.

Since leaving school Jex is much calmer and happier – but he is no angel! He has more interests than most 19 year olds. He has a vegetable garden and he is studying horticulture part-time. He loves walking his dog on the beach, he meditates. He uses public transport to travel all over the city to meet up with friends. He enjoys cooking, swimming, sketching. He paints – I once came home from work to find he'd painted his Labrador in the colours of his favourite football team!

Jex earned his PADI open water dive certification, we've swum with whale sharks, we've been hot air ballooning, we've back-packed through Asia. Jex loves his computer and webcam. He's a wiz with technology and gaming. His is a global world. He chats online with friends in Canada, Indonesia, New Zealand – often with four or five at a time.

Jex now has a girlfriend, Kirsty, and they are planning to move into their own home. Kirsty is the responsible one and Jex provides the entertainment!

And me? I met a wonderful man, David, who is also deaf. Jex adores him. I adore him. I am loved and I am blessed! I have experienced so much and have been stretched in all directions. Things change. What's overwhelming today will run its course. Life works out.

Jenny's email: jennytruran@hotmail.com

11

Ask for Help

People who get what they want, ask for it. It pays to ask!
- If you want to do a deal, ask.
- If you would like a job, ask.
- If you want a date, ask.
- If you are going through hard times and you need help, ask.

We can learn from kids! Kids are very good at asking and they don't quit... "Can I have an ice cream? Johnny has an ice cream. Can I have an ice cream like Johnny? Can I have an ice cream?"

Why are children so good at asking? Because a) they know exactly what they want, and b) they feel good about themselves. People with high self-esteem are able to ask for what they want. We need to be comfortable asking for these reasons:
- To live a good life you have to feel that you *deserve it*. As you ask – and receive – you develop an attitude of expectancy and so life continues to bless you.
- Asking is important for your health. When you don't ask, you often get overlooked, ignored, left out. That leads to frustration and a knot in your gut. Whenever you don't express yourself, your stomach keeps count.
- Asking is the first logical step in letting God, your boss, your family and friends know what you want.

Many people are more than willing to help if they can see that, a) you are in need, and b) you are already doing everything you can. By asking you give somebody else the pleasure of helping you. In fact, failing to ask is selfish. If you like to help others, then give them the same opportunity!

Tips when asking
Expect people to say "Yes"

If you expect to be rejected, you will be rejected. It's all about your attitude and your language. How would you expect people to answer the following questions?

"You wouldn't want to buy one would you?"
"No I wouldn't!"

"You can't help me can you?"
"No I can't."

"You can't upgrade my seat, can you?"
"Are you crazy?"

How much different does this sound?
- "Would you like to buy one?"
- "Can you help me?"
- "Can you please give me an upgrade?"

Be clear about what you want

If you let people know exactly what you want from them, you have a good chance of getting it. Specific requests get their attention. For example, "I would like an hour of your time on Saturday morning. Can you meet me at 10.30?" or "May I have a raise of £3,000?"

Persist

Let's imagine it's your dream to have a date with Lola. The first time you ask her out she says, "No." The next seven times she says, "No." The eighth time she says, "Let's go!" You have a wonderful romantic evening, Lola is captivated by your charm, you marry and live happily ever after.

So why did she finally say, "Yes"? Perhaps:

- she realised you were serious
- you caught her in a good mood
- her boyfriend dumped her (circumstances had changed)
- she did some research
- you got better at asking
- she admired your persistence
- she simply changed her mind.

There are a thousand reasons why a "No" becomes a "Yes."

Asking for Guidance

Anyone can receive inner guidance and inspiration. You don't have to be a paid-up member of your local church! Each of us can access help from a source higher

than our physical selves. Whether you are comfortable with words like *God, Source, Infinite Wisdom* is not an issue. But you need to be *seriously asking* and *seriously listening.* Inner communication is like regular communication between people. To get help, you need to be open to it.

Imagine that I wanted to get to the train station and I stopped you in the street to say, *"Can you tell me which way to the train station – actually I do know the way and I have found my own way there before very successfully, and I have some good reasons why I'm here and not there yet, and I don't really need anyone's help but I'm curious to see if you know as much as me – I'm doing fine actually and I can find it by myself..."*

Could you help me get to the station? Not likely. I'm justifying all my actions. I already have all the answers and I'm not listening anyway. My ego is in the way.

But what if I had been wandering the streets for three days and I staggered towards you thirsty and exhausted and said, *"How do I get to the station?"* Now I'm hungry for information. I'm making no excuses. I'm beyond worrying about what you think of me. My ego is out of the way. I'm in a state of complete non-resistance. Now I'm listening. Now you can help me.

In everyday life we can receive help only when we are open to it. So it is with inner guidance, inspiration, intuition. Do you have to be on your knees before you get inspiration? Not at all. THE EASIEST WAY TO GET INSPIRATION IS BY BEING HAPPY AND GRATEFUL. That's when life flows, that's when you get ideas when you want them and help when you need it.

Will I hear a voice from the sky?

When you are overwhelmed and distressed, your best strategy is to say, "Please show me the next step." If you are humble enough and open enough to say, "Just show me what I need to do today," and ask for the same help tomorrow, you can find your way out of the abyss.

Let's say that you are flat broke. You've lost your job, you're hungry, your car has been repossessed and you are facing eviction. You see no way out and so you decide to ask for divine guidance. Now, to you, the ideal solution might be first prize in the state lottery – but solutions may come in other ways. Very likely, help will be more of an unfolding process. Help doesn't mean that *everything is fixed for* us. Help means assistance and direction.

Ask and you will be shown but usually, it won't be a voice from the sky. It could be that a friend calls with a helpful suggestion; it could be that you are led to a book or a magazine article. It could be that for no known reason, you turn to a TV channel you never watch and see an advertisement you never saw before.

You say, "My problem is that I don't even know what I want!" Then ask for help. Ask to be shown and keep asking: "I want to know what I want! *Show me* what I want!" Answers will come.

Often we receive help and never recognise it. So we say, "It wasn't divine inspiration, it was actually my Uncle Ted who showed up unexpectedly." But in fact, Uncle Ted was a part of a miraculous process.

In a Nutshell

If we ask, we find help and guidance. As we make it a habit to silently give thanks, help and guidance come more and more often.

Finding Your Wallet, Finding Answers

How often do you lose something – your keys, your wallet, your phone – and search desperately without luck. Eventually you give up. You say to yourself, "If I quit looking, I will find it." You abandon your desperate search and get on with your day. And then, within minutes, and for absolutely no reason, you decide to shift a cushion on the three-piece suite and there, wedged into the armrest is your wallet.

The secret to finding solutions in your life is a lot like finding your wallet. You say to yourself, "I want to find it – I will find it" – and then you quit banging your head against a wall. You let go.

Needing versus Wanting

Wanting is an important part of the process. But it is a relaxed kind of *wanting* – not a desperate "This is ruining my life" kind of *needing*. Here is an important distinction: THE FEELING OF *NEEDING* IS TOTALLY DIFFERENT FROM THE FEELING OF *WANTING*. Needing is more like a *hopeless desperation*. When you need something, your attention is on what you *don't have.* And when you focus on what you don't have you will continue to have what you *don't have!*

Wanting is more of a *happy anticipation.* When you want something, you are focused on what you *will have.* That is why you get it.

Songwriters and inventors will often say, "The idea just came to me." Perhaps you have thought, "How come brilliant ideas don't come to me? I would like to invent something! I would like to write a hit song." When you really, really want ideas and inspiration they do come.

Paul McCartney, ex-Beatle and writer of the most recorded pop tune ever, said that the melody for "Yesterday" came to him in a dream. You say, "What a lucky guy! He takes a nap and wakes up having written the most popular tune in history. I'd like to do that!" But there is more to it. Here is a man whose every waking moment was dedicated to writing beautiful music. He spent his life combining words, phrases and melodies – pulling them apart and putting them back together. When you want something that much, you get inspiration.

The other half of the story is that he spent *months* writing the lyrics. So sometimes you get flashes of inspiration and sometimes you need to roll up your sleeves.

The secret to finding solutions – creative solutions, financial solutions, relationship solutions – is twofold: you have to *want it* and your mind needs to be in *a relaxed state of anticipation.*

Achieving Goals: is it more important to *want* or *believe?*

In 2004, Alicia Sorohan was camping in remote northern Australia when a 4.2 metre (13 foot), 300 kilo crocodile dragged her friend from a nearby tent. Alicia threw herself on the back of the crocodile and grabbed its head. Alicia was bitten in the scuffle but managed to save her friend. Ultimately Alicia's son arrived and shot the croc.

If you were to interview Alicia as she launched herself at the reptile, "Alicia, you weigh 50 kilos. How do you fancy your chances wrestling a 300 kilo crocodile which is arguably the most successful predator of the last 250 million years?" She'd likely say, "They're not good!" But Alicia *wanted so much* to help her friend.

We read about mothers who lift the back end of a truck to save their toddler from being crushed to death. They don't believe it is possible to lift a truck, but they *want it so much,* they do it anyway.

So sometimes, to achieve a goal, *wanting* is enough.

And what if you *believe* it but you don't *want* it? Fred gets influenza every time he takes a vacation. He doesn't want it but his unshakeable belief makes it happen. Susie believes her husband is going to have an affair. She doesn't want it, but if she believes it long enough, it will happen. So we can achieve something even if we don't want it.

Most often, we achieve our goals with a combination of belief and want.

Greg's Story

Growing up I was very fortunate...

My Mum was an alcoholic and my Dad took no interest in anything.

My two older brothers, Jim and Don, were heroin addicts and drug traffickers. Don was murdered and Jim died from drug abuse.

My parents split when I was 13 – and I went to live with Mum in a caravan. From the age of 15 I was mostly on my own.

Why was I fortunate? Because I learned a lot about life. My family was the perfect example of HOW NOT TO LIVE. My parents and my brothers were my motivation for a better future. I *was* fortunate – but good fortune doesn't necessarily mean life starts out easy.

> "*My family was the perfect example of HOW NOT TO LIVE*"

My parents slept in separate rooms and never spoke to each other. I figured that was just normal.

When I was very small my brothers were my heroes. Then they got into drugs and crime and I felt let down, shattered – and scared. Dealers would come to our home demanding money. I remember when Big Bob the local hit-man paid a visit. Peeking through my bedroom window I could see him and my brother Jim on the front lawn. Big Bob had an axe handle and suddenly he brought it crashing down across Jim's skull. Jim went down in a pool of blood.

The police also visited quite often, usually to arrest my brothers. Jim and Don were in and out of jail for burglary and trafficking. I was ashamed whenever my brothers made the TV news and ashamed that I spent my childhood visiting jails.

By the time I was 15, Mum had given up on life. She stayed in bed for weeks at a time. She told me, "You are old enough to look after yourself." I did my best to take care of her. I also did what I could to help Dad, who by now had a brain tumor. Dad insisted that education was a total waste of time – but I continued to study. I supported myself by working in an Asian restaurant as a kitchen hand and home delivery guy.

My life goals were based on what my family *wasn't*. I wanted to:
- be happier than my parents
- be healthier than my brothers
- become a devoted husband and a loving father, and
- go to university instead of jail.

It would have been easier to give up and blame them – but too costly. I have a simple philosophy that has helped me through: *if what you are doing isn't working try something else. You are never beaten until you quit.*

I remember my graduation ceremony when I received my chemistry degree – I was so proud, my feet barely touched the stage. Today I am an industrial chemist. I have a beautiful wife who is devoted to our two happy, healthy daughters – one is seven and the other is about to turn 11. We are a close family.

Though I made my own life, I carried a lot of resentment toward my Dad for his disinterest and toward my brothers for being idiots. So in 2008 I decided to hold a memorial ceremony in their honour. My wife and daughters, my parents-in-law and I went to their grave sites and I spoke about all the good things they had each achieved. I told my family how much I loved my Dad and brothers – and why I loved them. I cried like I had never cried before. It was a huge relief to let go of all that anger. A massive weight lifted from my shoulders and my heart. I came away feeling cleansed and much, much happier.

Every day I feel so grateful for what I have.

12

The Importance of Being Happy

At our local vegetable market there is a Thai girl who sells Asian desserts from a small stand. She is so excited about her black rice pudding that you just want to buy it. No matter that you take it home and leave it in the back of your refrigerator. You feel good just buying it.

This girl doesn't even try to *sell you*. She is so joyful, she is like a magnet. So we buy black rice pudding each Friday and toss it out the following week.

How do you bring about change in your life? Let's take an unusual angle. In school we learned about the animal, vegetable and mineral kingdoms. In summary:

- Minerals: for example, pebbles and rocks, are the least emotional and the least excitable. Pebbles are made up of dense and slow-moving energy. Consequently, a pebble has a fairly dull existence.
- Plants: they have a more interesting life than a pebble. A plant has a higher vibration. Science confirms that a cabbage is capable of feeling limited "emotion" – so your cabbages grow better when you talk to them.
- Animals: are more emotional than plants so they have a higher vibration again. A pig's life is more interesting. Pigs learn stuff, pigs have sex. A pig sees more action than a carrot.

The pattern is: when you have a higher vibration, you can make more things happen. Of course, humans operate at a higher vibration than pebbles, parsnips or pigs, so their lives move faster. Now stay with me because here is where all this makes sense...

Question: What *kind of people* stay stuck?

Answer: Emotionless people.

Why? You are a vibrational being in a vibrational universe. By your thoughts and your vibrations, you connect with everything around you. Through your feelings you attract opportunity. Emotion is the driving force behind your intentions.

Note the word: *"E-Motion."* People without emotions are like a car without gas – they have no motion! So people who never get excited stay stuck in a rut. When you have the enthusiasm of a piece of rock, you get a life experience to match. You've met those couldn't-care-less people – the walking dead. Their mantra is, "Everything is too hard. Nothing good ever happens." And they are right. For them, nothing much ever happens – but they are the reason nothing happens.

So what kinds of people make the most progress in the least time? People who:

• know what they want
• believe they deserve it, and
• are joyful and enthusiastic.

Who operate like this? Children.

See how perfect it is! As a child you didn't have to learn any of this. You arrived as a powerful package, armed with the tools to create and attract. When we stay childlike, life moves quickly.

- Two-year-olds know what they want.
- Two-year-olds believe they are beautiful and deserving.
- Two-year-olds are full of joy and emotion.

It all makes sense. When you are bored and discouraged, and you don't even know what you want, you stagnate – because thoughts without emotion are USELESS! As you rediscover your enthusiasm and EMOTION, your life accelerates.

HAPPY PEOPLE ARE NOT HAPPY BECAUSE THEY ARE SUCCESSFUL. THEY ARE SUCCESSFUL BECAUSE THEY ARE HAPPY.

You may recall happy times in your life when everything fell into place. You may know happy people who live charmed lives doing what they love, sailing from one wonderful opportunity to another.

It is not luck.

Twenty years ago I wrote a book, *Being Happy!* I thought then that happiness was a worthy goal. But I understand something now that I didn't know then.

HAPPINESS – *FEELING GOOD* – IS YOUR MOST IMPORTANT GOAL.

You create your life according to how you feel. When you *feel good* your entire being is in harmony with the world around you. As you face challenges, so you find solutions. You keep on finding yourself in the right place at the right time. It's not about your IQ. It's not about whether you are a sinner or a saint. It is about how you *feel*.

Your mission is to feel *as good as possible as often as possible*. These habits help:

1: Like Yourself:
Your most important relationship is with yourself. When you constantly criticise yourself, you sabotage your life. When you like yourself, you allow yourself to be happier, healthier and more prosperous. Be gentle with yourself.

2: Be Flexible:
Trying to control the world and judging everyone in it wears you out. Don't argue with what has *already happened*. Roll with the punches, enjoy life's surprises.

3: Focus on What You Want:
Picture yourself as you want to be, see your life as you want it.

4: Get Relaxed with Money:
Money is like a dog – when you chase it, it runs away. If you assume it doesn't like you, it will bite you on the bum. When you are comfortable with it, it will land in your lap.

5: Be Grateful:
No matter how little you have, focus on what you do have and more will come. Look for good things, always. You say, "When will I be happy?" When gratitude becomes a habit.

People say, "When I get what I want, I'll be happy!" but they have it back to front.

When you are happy, you get what you want.

Download Andrew Matthews' other books now!
www.andrewmatthews.com

We hope you enjoyed this Hay House book.
If you would like to receive a free catalogue featuring additional
Hay House books and products, or if you would like information
about the Hay Foundation, please contact:

Hay House UK Ltd
Astley House, 33 Notting Hill Gate, London W11 3JQ
Tel: +44 (0)20 3675 2450; Fax: +44 (0)20 3675 2451
www.hayhouse.co.uk • www.hayfoundation.org

***

Published and distributed in the United States of America by:
Hay House, Inc. • PO Box 5100 • Carlsbad, CA 92018-5100
Tel: (1) 760 431 7695 or (1) 800 654 5126;
Fax: (1) 760 431 6948 or (1) 800 650 5115
www.hayhouse.com

***

Published and distributed in Australia by:
Hay House Australia Ltd • 18/36 Ralph Street • Alexandria, NSW 2015
Tel: (61) 2 9669 4299, Fax: (61) 2 9669 4144
www.hayhouse.com.au

***

Published and distributed in the Republic of South Africa by:
Hay House SA (Pty) Ltd • PO Box 990 • Witkoppen 2068
Tel/Fax: (27) 11 467 8904
www.hayhouse.co.za

***

Published and distributed in India by:
Hay House Publishers India • Muskaan Complex • Plot No.3
B-2 • Vasant Kunj • New Delhi - 110 070
Tel: (91) 11 41761620; Fax: (91) 11 41761630
www.hayhouse.co.in

***

Distributed in Canada by:
Raincoast • 9050 Shaughnessy St • Vancouver, BC V6P 6E5
Tel: (1) 604 323 7100
Fax: (1) 604 323 2600

***

Sign up via the Hay House UK website to receive the Hay House
online newsletter and stay informed about what's going on with your
favourite authors. You'll receive bimonthly announcements
about discounts and offers, special events, product highlights,
free excerpts, giveaways, and more!
www.hayhouse.co.uk